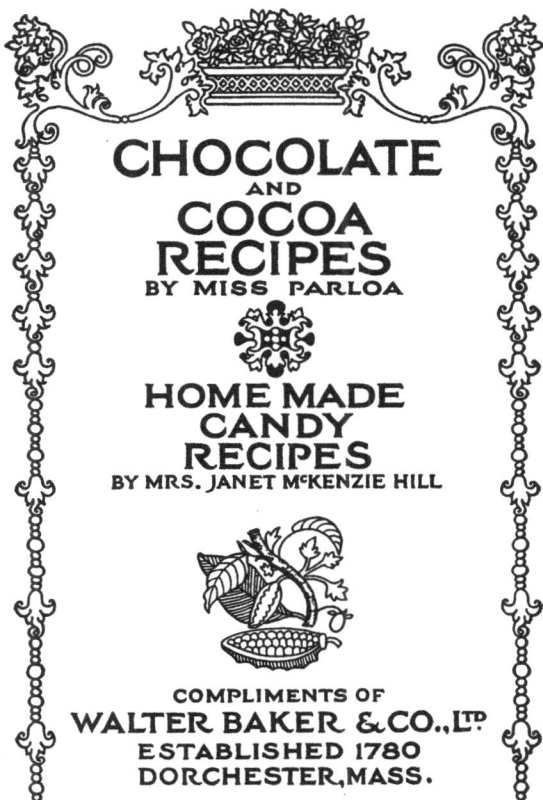

CHOCOLATE
AND
COCOA
RECIPES
BY MISS PARLOA

HOME MADE
CANDY
RECIPES
BY MRS. JANET McKENZIE HILL

COMPLIMENTS OF
WALTER BAKER & CO., LTD.
ESTABLISHED 1780
DORCHESTER, MASS.

COPYRIGHT, 1913
BY WALTER BAKER & CO., LTD.

BIRD'S-EYE VIEW OF WALTER BAKER & CO.'S MILLS, DORCHESTER AND MILTON, MASS.
FLOOR SPACE, OVER 14 ACRES.

THE STORY OF THE CHOCOLATE GIRL

HE famous picture of "La Belle Chocolatière," known all over the world as the trade-mark that distinguishes the Cocoa and Chocolate preparations made by Walter Baker & Co. Ltd., was the masterpiece of Jean-Etienne Liotard, a noted Swiss painter who was born in 1702 and died in 1790. It is one of the chief attractions in the Dresden Gallery, being better known and more sought after than any other work of art in that collection. There is a romance connected with the charming Viennese girl who served as the model, which is well worth telling. One of the leading journals of Vienna has thrown some light on the Baltauf, or Baldauf, family to which the subject of Liotard's painting belonged. Anna, or Annerl, as she was called by friends and relatives, was the daughter of Melchior Baltauf, a knight, who was living in Vienna in 1760, when Liotard was in that city making portraits of some members of the Austrian Court. It is not clear whether Anna was earning her living as a chocolate bearer at that time or whether she posed as a society belle in that becoming costume; but, be that as it may, her beauty won the love of a prince of the Empire, whose name, Dietrichstein, is known now only because he married the charming girl who was immortalized by a great artist. The marriage caused a great deal of talk in Austrian society at the time, and many different stories have been told about it. The prejudices of caste have always been very strong in Vienna, and a daughter of a knight, even if well-to-do, was not considered a suitable match for a member of the court. It is said that on the wedding day Anna invited the chocolate bearers with whom she had worked or played, and in "sportive joy at her own elevation" offered her hand to them saying, "Behold! now that I am a princess you may kiss my hand." She was probably about twenty years of age when the portrait was painted in 1760, and she lived until 1825.

It is pleasant to think of the graceful figure of the Chocolate Girl as it appears upon Walter Baker & Co.'s packages becoming associated with cocoa and chocolate preparations, as a positive guarantee of purity and fine quality.

The term "Cocoa," a corruption of "Cacao," is almost universally used in English-speaking countries to designate the seeds of the small tropical tree known to botanists as THEOBROMA CACAO, from which a great variety of preparations under the name of cocoa and chocolate for eating and drinking are made. The name "Chocolate" is nearly the same in most European languages, and is taken from the Mexican name of the drink, "Chocolatl" or "Cacahuatl." The Spaniards found chocolate in common use among the Mexicans at the time of the invasion under Cortez, in 1519, and it was introduced into Spain immediately after. The Mexicans not only used chocolate as a staple article of food, but they used the seeds of the cacao tree as a medium of exchange.

No better evidence could be offered of the great advance which has been made in recent years in the knowledge of dietetics than the remarkable increase in the consumption of cocoa and chocolate in this country. The amount retained for home consumption in 1860 was only 1,181,054 pounds—about 3-5 of an ounce for each inhabitant. The amount retained for home consumption for the year 1913 was approximately 150,542,904 pounds — about 25 ounces for each inhabitant.

Although there was a marked increase in the consumption of tea and coffee during the same period, the ratio of increase fell far below that of cocoa. It is evident that the coming American is going to be less of a tea and coffee drinker, and more of a cocoa and chocolate drinker. This is the natural result of a better knowledge of the laws of health, and of the food value of a beverage which nourishes the body while it also stimulates the brain.

Baron von Liebig, one of the best-known writers on dietetics, says:

"It is a perfect food, as wholesome as delicious, a beneficent restorer of exhausted power; but its quality must be good and it must be carefully prepared. It is highly nourishing and easily digested, and is fitted to repair wasted strength, preserve health, and prolong life. It agrees with dry temperaments and convalescents; with mothers who nurse their children; with those whose occupations oblige them to undergo severe mental strains; with public speakers, and with all those who give to work a portion of the time needed for sleep. It soothes both stomach and brain, and for this reason, as well as for others, it is the best friend of those engaged in literary pursuits."

The three associated beverages, cocoa, tea, and coffee, are known to the French as *aromatic* drinks. Each of these has its characteristic aroma. The fragrance and flavor are so marked that they cannot be imitated by any artificial product, although numerous attempts have been made in regard to all three. Hence the detection of adulteration is not a difficult matter. Designing persons, aware of the extreme difficulty of

4

imitating these substances, have undertaken to employ lower grades, and, by manipulation, copy, as far as may be, the higher sorts. Every one knows how readily tea, and coffee, for that matter, will take up odors and flavors from substances placed near them. This is abundantly exemplified in the country grocery or general store, where the teas and coffees share in the pervasive fragrance of the cheese and kerosene. But perhaps it is not so widely understood that some of these very teas and coffees had been artificially flavored or corrected before they reached their destination in this country.

Cocoa lends itself very readily to such preliminary treatment. In a first-class article, the beans should be of the highest excellence; they should be carefully grown on the plantation and there prepared with great skill, arriving in the factory in good condition. In the factory they should simply receive the mechanical treatment requisite to develop their high and attractive natural flavor and fragrance. They should be most carefully shelled after roasting and finely ground without concealed additions. This is the process in all honest manufactories of the cocoa products.

R. Whymper, in his recent work, ''Cocoa and Chocolate, Their Chemistry and Manufacture,'' says: ''It is our experience that the chocolate of finest flavor is prepared by using the best quality beans, properly roasted, without any further treatment.''

Now, as a matter of fact, in the preparation of many of the cocoa products on the market, a wholly different course has been pursued. Beans of poor quality are used, because of their cheapness, and in some instances they are only imperfectly, if at all, shelled before grinding. Chemical treatment is relied on to correct in part the odor and taste of such inferior goods, and artificial flavors, other than the time-honored natural vanilla and the like, are added freely. The detection of such imposition is easy enough to the expert, but it is difficult to the novice; therefore the public is largely unable to discriminate between the good and the inferior, and it is perforce compelled to depend almost entirely on the character and reputation of the manufacturer.

''A well-known medical expert has said: ''*The treatment of cocoa with potash is to be strongly condemned, as the slightly increased solubility obtained is more than counterbalanced by the injurious effects of the chemical upon the system, and those who value good health would be well advised to leave such cocoas alone.*''

A distinguished London physician, in giving some hints concerning the proper preparation of cocoa, says:

5

"Start with a pure cocoa of undoubted quality and excellence of manufacture, and which bears the name of a respectable firm. This point is important, for there are many cocoas on the market which have been doctored by the addition of alkali, starch, malt, kola, hops, etc."

Baker's Breakfast Cocoa is absolutely pure, and, being ground to an extraordinary degree of fineness, is highly soluble. The analyst of the Massachusetts State Board of Health states in his recent valuable work on "Food Inspection and Analysis," that the treatment of cocoa with alkali for the purpose of producing a more perfect emulsion is objectionable, even if not considered as a form of adulteration. Cocoa thus treated is generally darker in color than the pure article. The legitimate means, he says, for making it as soluble as possible, is to pulverize it very fine, so that particles remain in even suspension and form a smooth paste.

That is the way the Baker Cocoa is treated. It has received the Grand Prize—the highest award ever given in this country, and altogether 53 highest awards in Europe and America.

Suggestions Relative to the Cooking of Chocolate and Cocoa

BY MRS. ELLEN H. RICHARDS

OF THE MASSACHUSETTS INSTITUTE OF TECHNOLOGY

The flavor of the cocoa bean seems to be almost universally liked, and the use of the various preparations made from it is constantly increasing. From the sweet chocolate with which the traveler now provides himself in all journeys in which the supply of food is doubtful either in quantity or quality, to delicate covering and flavoring of cakes and ices, nearly all kinds of culinary preparations have benefited by the abundance of this favorite substance.

In these forms, chocolate is used in a semi-raw state, the bean having been simply roasted at a gentle heat, ground and mixed with sugar, which holds the fat. By varying the quantity of the chocolate to be mixed with the ingredients of the cake or ice, an unlimited variety of flavors can be obtained.

6

In preparing it as a beverage for the table a mistake has been frequently made in considering chocolate merely as a flavor, an adjunct to the rest of the meal, instead of giving it its due prominence as a real food, containing all the necessary nutritive principles. A cup of chocolate made with sugar and milk is in itself a fair breakfast.

There is much to be said in favor of preparations of the whole bean which secure all of the valuable nutrition contained in this "food for the gods," and, rightly understood, it is possible to make them more important articles of diet than they now are. But since the large percentage of fat seems to require correspondingly large quantities of sugar to render the beverage palatable, and this very rich, sweet drink soon cloys if made strong enough to be nutritious, it is, fortunately, possible to extract the larger part of the fat without injury to the flavor so characteristic of chocolate. In this form, called cocoa, less sugar and more milk are needed, and the resulting beverage suits even delicate stomachs and is yet of high food value.

It is the object of all cooking to render raw material more palatable and more nutritious, and therefore more digestible. The cooking of cocoa and chocolate is no exception to this rule. Certain extractive principles are soluble only in water which has reached the boiling point; and the starch, which the seed contains, is swollen only at this temperature.

Chocolate or cocoa is not properly cooked by having boiling water poured over it. It is true that as the whole powder is in suspension and is swallowed, its food material can be assimilated as it is when the prepared chocolate is eaten raw; but in order to bring out the full, fine flavor and to secure the most complete digestibility, the preparation, whatever it be, should be subjected to the boiling point for a few minutes. In this all connoisseurs are agreed.

CHOICE RECIPES

BY

MISS MARIA PARLOA

SPECIALLY PREPARED FOR

WALTER BAKER & CO., LTD.

AND REDUCED BY MISS FANNIE MERRITT FARMER TO LEVEL MEASUREMENTS TO MEET THE NEEDS OF PRESENT-DAY DEMANDS

WALTER BAKER & CO.'S BREAKFAST COCOA

3 tablespoons Breakfast Cocoa,	Few grains salt,
3 tablespoons sugar,	1 cup boiling water,
3 cups milk.	

Scald milk in double-boiler. Mix cocoa, sugar, and salt and add water gradually, that mixture may be perfectly smooth; bring to boiling point and let boil three minutes. Pour into scalded milk and beat two minutes, using a wire whisk or Dover egg beater, thus preventing scum, which is so unsightly. This process is called milling.

RECEPTION COCOA

Make same as Breakfast Cocoa, and serve in place of Hot Chocolate at afternoon teas or receptions, accompanied by whipped cream, sweetened and flavored with vanilla. Flavor cocoa with one-half teaspoon vanilla, two teaspoons brandy or one-fourth teaspoon cinnamon. To offer variety, in place of whipped cream use one marshmallow to each cup, pouring cocoa over it. The cheapest grade must be used, as the more expensive ones do not melt.

HOT CHOCOLATE

2 ounces Walter Baker & Co.'s Premium No. 1 Chocolate,	
Few grains salt,	1 quart milk,
¾ cup boiling water,	⅓ cup sugar,
1 teaspoon cornstarch.	

Thoroughly mix sugar and cornstarch, and dilute with one-half cup cold milk. Scald remaining milk in double-boiler, add mixture and cook ten minutes, stirring constantly until mixture thickens slightly. Melt chocolate in small saucepan, placed in larger saucepan of boiling water, and add gradually boiling water and salt. Add to milk mixture, and beat until frothy, using a wire whisk or egg beater, thus preventing scum, which is so unsightly. Serve in chocolate cups, with whipped cream, sweetened and flavored with vanilla. If a thinner drink is desired omit cornstarch.

A sufficient quantity to allow for six people.

HOT CHOCOLATE
(Made from Condensed Milk)

2 squares Walter Baker & Co.'s Premium No. 1 Chocolate
⅓ cup sugar,
Few grains salt,
1 Chocolate
1 quart boiling water,
1 small can evaporated milk.

Melt chocolate in saucepan, placed over larger saucepan of boiling water; then add sugar and salt. Pour on, gradually, boiling water; again bring to the boiling point, and let boil five minutes. Add milk, mill, and boil two minutes.

VIENNA CHOCOLATE

3 ounces Walter Baker & Co.'s Vanilla Chocolate,
Few grains salt,
1 quart milk.

Put milk in double-boiler, add chocolate broken in pieces, and stir until chocolate has melted and milk has reached the scalding point. Add salt, and beat until frothy. Serve in chocolate cups, with whipped cream sweetened and flavored with vanilla.

If the sweetened chocolate is not at hand, unsweetened may be used in its stead, with the addition of one-third cup of sugar and one teaspoon vanilla.

CHOCOLATE SYRUP

⅓ cup Walter Baker & Co.'s Breakfast Cocoa,
2 cups sugar,
1 cup boiling water.

Mix cocoa and sugar thoroughly. Add water gradually while stirring constantly, bring to the boiling point, and let boil five minutes. Cool, add one-half tablespoon vanilla. Store in glass jar and keep in a cold place.

CHOCOLATE MILK SHAKE

¼ cup finely crushed ice,
2 tablespoons Chocolate Syrup,
½ cup milk,
¼ cup Apollinaris water or soda water drawn from syphon.

Put ice in tumbler, add remaining ingredients, and shake until well mixed. Serve with or without whipped cream, sweetened and flavored.

CHOCOLATE ICE-CREAM SODA

Put a small portion of ice-cream in tumbler, add two tablespoons chocolate syrup, and fill glass with ice-cold soda water, drawn from syphon.

MILTON PUDDING

2 cups stale bread crumbs,
4 cups scalded milk,
2 squares Walter Baker & Co.'s Premium No. 1 Chocolate,
⅓ cup sugar,
2 eggs,
½ teaspoon salt,
½ teaspoon cinnamon.

Soak bread in milk one-half hour. Melt chocolate in saucepan placed over hot water; add sugar, mixed with cinnamon and salt, and enough milk — taken from bread and milk — to make of consistency to pour. Add to bread mixture; then add eggs, beaten slightly. Turn into a slightly-buttered pudding-dish, and bake in a moderate oven forty-five minutes. Serve with egg or vanilla cream sauce.

EGG SAUCE

Whites two eggs,
1 cup powdered sugar,
Yolks two eggs.
1 cup heavy cream,
1 teaspoon vanilla,

Beat whites of eggs until stiff and dry, and add gradually, while beating constantly, sugar; then add yolks of eggs, beaten until thick and lemon-colored, and vanilla. Cut and fold in cream beaten until stiff.

VANILLA CREAM SAUCE

¼ cup butter,
⅔ cup powdered sugar,
1 teaspoon vanilla,
1½ cups heavy cream.

Work butter until creamy and add sugar gradually, while beating constantly, and vanilla; then add heavy cream beaten until stiff. Place bowl in saucepan of boiling water and stir constantly three minutes. Pour into a warm bowl and serve at once.

CHOCOLATE MERINGUE PUDDING

2 cups milk,
¼ cup cornstarch,
1 ounce Walter Baker & Co.'s Premium
 No. 1 Chocolate,
2 eggs,
½ cup powdered sugar,
¼ teaspoon salt,
½ teaspoon vanilla.

Mix cornstarch with one-half cup milk. Scald remaining milk with chocolate. Add cornstarch mixture gradually, while stirring constantly, and cook fifteen minutes. Beat yolks of eggs and add sugar, reserving two tablespoons. Pour hot mixture gradually, while stirring constantly, on egg mixture and add salt. Turn into a buttered pudding dish and bake twenty minutes in a moderate oven. Beat whites of eggs until stiff and add gradually, while beating constantly, reserved sugar. Spread meringue on pudding and cook in a slow oven ten minutes. Serve either hot or cold.

CHOCOLATE SOUFFLÉ

2 tablespoons butter,
3 tablespoons flour,
1 cup milk,
⅓ cup sugar,
2 tablespoons boiling water,
4 eggs,
2 ounces Walter Baker & Co.'s Premium No. 1 Chocolate.

Melt butter, add flour and stir until well blended, then pour on gradually the milk and bring to the boiling point. Melt chocolate in small saucepan, placed in larger saucepan of boiling water; add sugar and water and stir until smooth.

10

Combine mixtures and add yolks of eggs beaten until thick and lemon-colored. Cool and fold in whites of eggs beaten until stiff. Turn into a buttered pudding-dish, and bake in a moderate oven from thirty to thirty-five minutes. Serve at once with vanilla cream sauce. (See page 10.)

CHOCOLATE BLANC = MANGE

1 quart milk,	¼ cup sugar,
1 tablespoon Sea Moss Farina,	2 tablespoons boiling water,
2 ounces Walter Baker & Co.'s Premium	1 teaspoon vanilla,
No. 1 Chocolate,	¼ teaspoon salt.

Put milk in double-boiler, place on range, and while milk is still cold sprinkle in farina, stirring constantly. Cover and cook twenty minutes, stirring frequently. Melt chocolate over hot water, add sugar and boiling water. When smooth add to milk with vanilla and salt. Strain into a mould first dipped in cold water. Set mould in cold place, not moving until blanc-mange is cold and firm. Serve with sugar and cream. If moulded for individual service, use an additional one-half cup milk.

CHOCOLATE PUDDING

1 quart milk,	¼ teaspoon salt,
⅓ cup cornstarch,	2 ounces Walter Baker & Co.'s Pre-
2 eggs,	mium No. 1 Chocolate,
½ cup powdered sugar,	½ cup granulated sugar.

Mix cornstarch with one-half cup cold milk. Scald remaining milk, with chocolate and one-half cup sugar, and add cornstarch mixture gradually, while stirring constantly, and let cook fifteen minutes. Beat eggs until light, and add, gradually, sugar and salt. Stir into hot mixture and cook ten minutes. Pour into individual moulds, first dipped in cold water, and chill thoroughly. Remove from moulds to serving-dish, arranging in the form of a circle. Pile in centre whipped cream sweetened and flavored with vanilla.

BAKED CHOCOLATE CUSTARD

2 cups milk,	2 eggs,
1 inch-piece stick cinnamon,	1 tablespoon boiling water,
1 ounce Walter Baker & Co.'s Premium	¼ teaspoon salt,
No. 1 Chocolate,	5 tablespoons sugar.

Scald milk with cinnamon. Melt chocolate; add three tablespoons sugar and boiling water. Stir until smooth; then add to scalded milk. Beat eggs slightly, add remaining sugar and salt. Combine mixtures, and strain into slightly-buttered cups. Set in pan of hot water, and bake in a slow oven until firm, which may be determined by running a silver knife through custard. If knife comes out clean, custard is done.

SNOW PUDDING
(Chocolate Sauce)

2½ cups milk,
⅓ cup cornstarch,
⅓ teaspoon salt,

Whites 4 eggs,
½ cup powdered sugar,
1 teaspoon vanilla.

Mix cornstarch and salt with one-half cup milk. Scald remaining milk; add cornstarch mixture gradually, while stirring constantly, and let cook fifteen minutes. Beat whites of eggs until stiff, and then gradually, while beating constantly, add sugar and vanilla. Add to cooked mixture, and beat vigorously one minute. Turn into a mould, first dipped in cold water; chill, remove from mould, and serve with

CHOCOLATE SAUCE

2 cups milk,
2 ounces Walter Baker & Co.'s Premium
   No. 1 Chocolate,
Sugar,

Yolks 4 eggs,
⅛ teaspoon salt,
½ teaspoon vanilla.

Put chocolate, one-fourth cup sugar, and cold milk into double-boiler, and cook until milk is scalded. Mix yolks of eggs with one-third cup sugar and salt, and beat eight minutes. Pour milk gradually, while beating constantly, onto egg mixture; return to double-boiler and stir constantly until mixture thickens.

Strain, cool, and flavor with vanilla. This sauce may accompany cornstarch pudding, bread pudding, or cold cabinet pudding, or may be served in small glasses with whipped cream sweetened and flavored.

CHOCOLATE CREAM

¾ box gelatine, or
3 tablespoons granulated gelatine,
1 cup cold water,
1 quart milk,
2 ounces Walter Baker & Co.'s Premium
   No. 1 Chocolate,

¼ cup sugar,
2 tablespoons boiling water,
¼ teaspoon salt,
Yolks 5 eggs,
½ cup sugar,
2 teaspoons vanilla.

Soak gelatine in cold water twenty minutes. Scald milk. Melt chocolate over hot water, add sugar, boiling water and salt. Stir until smooth and add to milk. Beat egg yolks until thick, and add gradually, while beating constantly, one-half cup sugar. Add gradually to hot mixture, and cook until mixture thickens; then add gelatine and vanilla. Strain into mould first dipped in cold water, chill, and serve with sugar and cream.

CHOCOLATE CREAM RENVERSÉ

1 quart milk,
1 ounce Walter Baker & Co.'s Premium
   No. 1 Chocolate,

1 cup sugar,
7 eggs,
½ teaspoon salt.

Caramelize one-third cup sugar, turn into a hot charlotte russe mould, and turn the mould around and around until coated with the caramel. Scald milk with chocolate. Beat eggs slightly; add remaining sugar and salt. Pour milk slowly onto egg mixture, and strain into mould. Set in pan of hot water and bake in a slow oven until firm. Chill thoroughly, remove from mould, and serve with whipped cream sweetened and flavored with vanilla.

CHOCOLATE BAVARIAN CREAM

¼ package gelatine, or
1 tablespoon granulated gelatine,
Whip from 3 cups cream,
¼ cup cold water,

1½ ounces Walter Baker & Co.'s
    Premium No. 1 Chocolate,
2 tablespoons hot water,
½ cup sugar,
Few grains salt.

Soak gelatine in cold water twenty minutes. Melt chocolate, add sugar and hot water. Combine mixtures, and add one-third cup scalded cream which has drained from whip, and salt. As soon as gelatine has dissolved, set bowl containing mixture in pan of ice-water, and stir constantly until mixture begins to thicken, scraping from bottom and sides of bowl that it may not become lumpy. Stir in one-half the whip, and, when well-mixed, fold in remaining whip. Turn into a three-pint mould, sparingly greased with olive oil, spread evenly, and chill. By using the oil the cream may be easily removed from the mould. Heavy cream diluted with milk may be used in place of thin cream.

CHOCOLATE CHARLOTTE

¼ box of gelatine, or
1 tablespoon granulated gelatine,
¼ cup cold water,
½ ounce Walter Baker & Co.'s Premium
    No. 1 Chocolate,

¼ cup granulated sugar,
½ cup hot milk,
½ cup powdered sugar,
1 pint heavy cream,
Few grains salt,
6 lady fingers.

Soak gelatine in cold water and dissolve in scalded milk. Melt chocolate and add granulated sugar. Combine mixtures and strain into bowl. Set in pan of ice-water, and stir constantly until mixture begins to thicken; then add cream mixed with powdered sugar and salt and beaten until stiff, using a Dover egg-beater. Turn into a charlotte mould lined with lady fingers, and chill thoroughly.

CHOCOLATE ICE-CREAM

3 cups milk,
3 tablespoons flour,
2 cups sugar,
2 eggs,

¼ teaspoon salt,
2½ ounces Walter Baker & Co.'s Premium No. 1 Chocolate,
2 tablespoons hot water,
1 quart thin cream.

Scald milk. Mix flour and one-half the sugar and add eggs, slightly beaten, and salt. Add gradually to scalded milk, stirring constantly until mixture thickens, and afterwards occasionally, cooking twenty minutes. Melt chocolate over hot water, add one-fourth cup of the reserved sugar, and hot water. Stir until smooth, and add to cooked mixture. Strain, and add remaining sugar and cream. Cool and freeze, using three parts finely-crushed ice to one part rock salt.

CHOCOLATE MOUSSE

4½ cups thin cream,	¾ tablespoon granulated gelatine,
2 ounces Walter Baker & Co.'s	3 tablespoons boiling water,
Premium No. 1 Chocolate,	¾ cup granulated sugar,
½ cup powdered sugar,	1 teaspoon vanilla.

Place whip churn in bowl containing cream, and work with a quick downward and slow upward motion, removing whip as it forms to purée strainer placed over bowl, and continue whipping until cream comes below perforations in churn. Melt chocolate, add powdered sugar, and gradually the cream that would not whip, together with the cream drained from whip cream. Stir over fire until boiling point is reached, then add gelatine dissolved in boiling water, granulated sugar, and vanilla. Strain cooked mixture into a bowl set in pan of ice water. Stir constantly until mixture thickens, then fold in whip from cream. Turn into a chilled mould, fill to overflowing, cover with buttered paper (buttered side up), adjust cover, pack in salt and ice, using two parts finely crushed ice to one part rock salt, and let stand four hours. It will be necessary to turn off the water and repack before the freezing is accomplished.

CHOCOLATE COOKIES

½ cup butter,	2 ounces melted Walter Baker & Co.'s
1 tablespoon lard,	Premium No. 1 Chocolate,
1 cup sugar,	1 egg,
¼ teaspoon salt,	½ teaspoon soda,
1 teaspoon cinnamon,	2 tablespoons milk,
	2½ cups flour.

Cream the butter, add lard and cream together; then add gradually, while beating constantly, sugar, salt, cinnamon and chocolate. When thoroughly blended, add egg well beaten, soda dissolved in milk, and flour. Chill, toss on a slightly floured board, roll one-eighth inch in thickness, shape with a small round cutter first dipped in flour, arrange on a buttered tin sheet, and bake in a moderate oven.

CHOCOLATE WAFERS

4 ounces Walter Baker & Co.'s	Yolks 6 eggs,
Premium No. 1 Chocolate,	1 cup sugar,
¼ cup flour,	Rind of ½ lemon,
¼ teaspoon cinnamon,	Juice of ½ lemon,
¼ teaspoon clove,	Whites 6 eggs,
	¼ teaspoon baking powder.

Grate chocolate and mix with flour, spices and baking powder. Beat yolks of eggs until thick and lemon-colored and add gradually, while beating constantly, the sugar; then add lemon rind and juice and beat five minutes. Combine mixtures and cut and fold in whites of eggs beaten until stiff and dry. Turn into buttered shallow pans, having mixture one-fourth inch in thickness, and bake in a slow oven. Remove from pans, cool, and put between layers currant jelly beaten with a fork until of right consistency to spread evenly. Cover with vanilla icing and, when set, mark in squares.

CHOCOLATE BISCUIT

Yolks 4 eggs,	Whites 4 eggs,
½ cup powdered sugar,	¾ cup flour,
1 ounce melted Walter Baker & Co.'s	Few grains salt.
Premium No. 1 Chocolate,	

Beat egg yolks until thick and add gradually, while beating constantly, the sugar. Cut and fold in chocolate, then flour mixed with salt, and lastly whites of eggs beaten until stiff. If the ingredients are stirred in rather than cut and folded in, the results will not be as satisfactory. Drop by teaspoons, one inch apart, on a paper brushed over with clarified butter, then dredged with powdered sugar and placed on a tin sheet; then sift over cakes powdered sugar.

Bake in a slow oven fifteen minutes. The mixture may be shaped same as lady fingers if preferred.

CHOCOLATE GINGERBREAD

1 cup molasses,	1 teaspoon ginger,
½ cup sour milk,	1 teaspoon cinnamon,
1 teaspoon soda,	½ teaspoon salt,
1 teaspoon cold water,	2 cups flour,
3 tablespoons melted butter,	2 ounces melted Walter Baker & Co.'s
	Premium No. 1 Chocolate.

Mix molasses and sour milk, and add two tablespoons butter and soda dissolved in cold water; then add flour mixed and sifted with spices and salt. Add chocolate and remaining butter. Pour into three buttered round layer cake tins (Washington Pie pans) and bake in a moderate oven twenty minutes. Remove from pans, cool, and cover with vanilla or chocolate icing.

VANILLA ICING

White 1 large egg,	1 cup confectioner's sugar,
	½ teaspoon vanilla.

Put egg white in bowl and add gradually, while stirring constantly, sugar. Beat three minutes, add vanilla and spread thinly on cake.

CHOCOLATE ICING

To vanilla icing add one tablespoon cold water. Melt one ounce Walter Baker & Co.'s Premium No. 1 Chocolate, and add one-fourth cup confectioner's sugar and one tablespoon hot water. Place over fire, stir until smooth and add another tablespoon hot water; then add to vanilla icing.

CHOCOLATE CAKE

½ cup butter,	3 eggs,
¾ cup sugar,	3 ounces Walter Baker & Co.'s
½ cup milk,	Premium No. 1 Chocolate,
½ teaspoon vanilla,	1¾ cups bread flour,

3 teaspoons baking powder.

Cream butter, add gradually sugar, milk, vanilla, eggs well beaten, chocolate melted, and flour mixed and sifted with baking powder. Turn into buttered shallow cake pans and bake from thirty to thirty-five minutes in a moderate oven.

CHOCOLATE GLACÉ CAKE

½ cup butter,	½ cup milk,
1 cup sugar,	1½ cups flour,
1 ounce Walter Baker & Co.'s	3 teaspoons baking powder,
Premium No. 1 Chocolate,	1 teaspoon vanilla.
2 eggs,	

Cream butter and add sugar gradually, while beating constantly; then add chocolate melted and unbeaten eggs. Beat vigorously five minutes, then add milk and flour mixed and sifted with baking powder, and vanilla. Turn into a buttered and floured shallow cake pan and bake in a moderate oven thirty-five minutes. Remove from pan and spread with

GLACÉ FROSTING

½ cup sugar,	3 tablespoons water,
	½ teaspoon vanilla.

Put sugar and water in small saucepan, place on range, stir until sugar is dissolved, bring to boiling point and boil without stirring until syrup when tried in cold water will form a ball of jelly-like consistency. Turn into a bowl, cool, then beat, using a wooden spoon until mixture is thick and white. Put bowl in saucepan of boiling water, and stir until icing is thin enough to pour; then add vanilla. Pour over cake and spread.

CHOCOLATE GLACÉ FROSTING

To glacé frosting add one ounce melted Walter Baker & Co.'s Premium No. 1 Chocolate and one tablespoon boiling water.

CHOCOLATE MARBLE CAKE

½ cup butter,	Whites 6 eggs,
1 cup sugar,	1 teaspoon vanilla,
½ cup milk,	2½ teaspoons baking powder,
1½ cups flour,	1 square Walter Baker & Co.'s
1 tablespoon flour,	Premium No. 1 Chocolate.

Cream butter and add sugar gradually; then add milk alternately with flour mixed and sifted with two teaspoons baking powder, whites of eggs beaten until stiff and dry, and vanilla. To one-third of the mixture add melted chocolate and reserved baking powder, mixed and sifted with remaining

CHOCOLATE PARFAIT
(See Page 29)

CHOCOLATE ÉCLAIRS
(See Page 17)

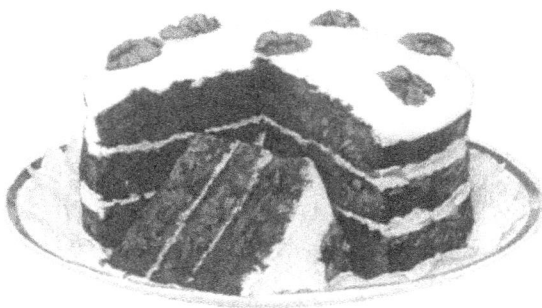

CHOCOLATE LAYER CAKE
(See Page 28.)

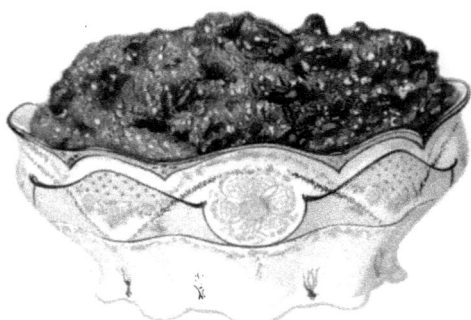

CHOCOLATE WHIP.
(See Page 30.)

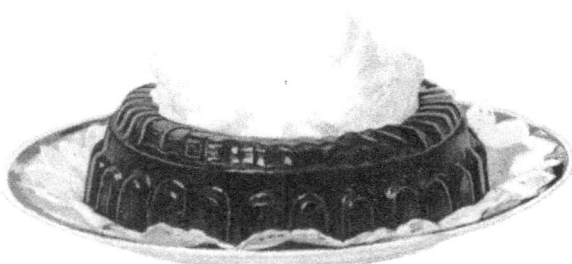

CHOCOLATE JELLY.
(See Page 30.)

CHOCOLATE HEARTS.
(See Page 36.)

flour. Butter a deep cake or angel cake pan, put in mixtures by spoonfuls, and bake in a moderate oven fifty minutes.

CHOCOLATE ÉCLAIRS

⅓ cup butter,   2 tablespoons sugar,
1 cup milk,   4 eggs,
                           1 cup flour.

Put butter, milk and sugar in saucepan. Bring to the boiling point, and add flour all at once and stir vigorously, using a wooden spoon. Remove from range as soon as mixture cleaves to spoon. Cool and add four eggs, one at a time, beating two minutes between the addition of each egg and five minutes after eggs are added. Shape mixture on a slightly buttered sheet four and one-half inches long by one inch wide, by forcing through a pastry tube; they should be one inch apart to allow for spreading. Bake in a moderate oven about twenty-five minutes. If removed from oven before they are thoroughly cooked, they will fall.

Cool, make a cut in the side of each without breaking apart, and fill with either of the following preparations.

CREAM FILLING No. I

To one cup heavy cream add four tablespoons sugar, one-half teaspoon vanilla and a few grains salt. Beat until stiff, using an egg beater or wire whisk.

CREAM FILLING No. II

Scald one and one-half cups milk. Mix three and one-half tablespoons flour with three-fourths cup sugar and one-eighth teaspoon salt, and add two eggs slightly beaten. Combine mixtures and cook in double-boiler fifteen minutes, stirring constantly until thickened, afterwards occasionally. Cool and flavor with one-half teaspoon vanilla.

ICING FOR ÉCLAIRS

1 cup sugar,   1 ounce Walter Baker & Co.'s Premium
5 tablespoons cold water,   No. 1 Chocolate.

Put sugar and water in saucepan, stir until sugar is dissolved, and cook without stirring until mixture, when tried in cold water, will form a syrup thick enough to coat the finger but not thick enough to form a jelly-like ball. Turn on a platter, let stand until cooled slightly, then stir with a wooden spoon until white and creamy. Add melted chocolate and stir until mixed. Put in saucepan placed over larger saucepan of boiling water, and beat until of right consistency to spread. To coat éclairs, it is best to apply icing with a butter brush.

CHOCOLATE PROFITEROLES

Make a paste same as for éclairs, using one-third cup sugar instead of three tablespoons. Add to paste while hot one ounce melted Walter Baker & Co.'s Premium No. 1 Chocolate. Cool and add eggs. Drop by spoonfuls on a slightly buttered tin sheet one and one-half inches apart, and shape with the handle of a wooden spoon as nearly circular as possible, having mixture slightly piled in centre. Bake in a moderate oven twenty-five to thirty minutes. Cool, split and fill same as éclairs.

CREAM CHOCOLATE CARAMELS

3 tablespoons butter,	1 cup heavy cream,
1 cup sugar,	¼ lb. Walter Baker & Co.'s Premium No. 1 Chocolate.
1 cup molasses,	

Melt butter and add sugar, molasses and cream. Bring to the boiling point, add chocolate, and stir constantly until chocolate has melted, and afterwards occasionally. Let boil until mixture will form a firm ball when tried in cold water. Turn into a buttered tin (square) pan, cool slightly, and cut in cubes. When cold, wrap in paraffine paper.

Three-fourths cup cut nut meats may be added to this recipe.

GENESSEE CARAMELS

Dip cream chocolate caramels in melted Walter Baker & Co.'s Dot Chocolate. Remove to oiled paper and let stand until chocolate is cool.

SUGAR CHOCOLATE CARAMELS

3 tablespoons butter,	¾ cup cream,
2¼ cups sugar,	3 ounces Walter Baker & Co.'s Premium No. 1 Chocolate.
1 tablespoon vanilla,	

Melt butter in granite-ware saucepan and add two cups sugar and cream. When boiling point is reached, add chocolate. Stir constantly until chocolate is melted, and afterwards occasionally. Let boil until a firm ball may be formed when tried in cold water. Stir in remaining sugar and vanilla. Pour into a buttered pan, having mixture three-fourths inch deep. Cool and mark in squares.

CHOCOLATE CREAMS I

White 1 egg,	1 lb. confectioner's sugar,
½ tablespoon cold water,	¾ teaspoon vanilla,
Walter Baker & Co.'s Dot Chocolate.	

Put egg, water, and vanilla in a bowl, and beat until well blended; then add gradually, while stirring constantly, sugar. Make into small balls, drop on a slightly-buttered paper, and let stand one hour. Melt five ounces Walter Baker & Co.'s Dot Chocolate in saucepan placed over hot water, and beat one minute. Drop balls, separately, in chocolate, and when coated remove to slightly-buttered paper, using a two-tined fork or confectioner's dipper.

It will be necessary to reheat chocolate during the dipping. Let stand in a cool, dry place to harden chocolate. If a small egg is used it will not take up all the sugar.

CHOCOLATE CREAMS II

2 cups sugar,	½ teaspoon glycerine,
⅛ teaspoon cream of tartar,	½ cup water,

Walter Baker & Co.'s Dot Chocolate.

Put ingredients (except chocolate) in a smooth granite-ware saucepan; place on range, stir until sugar is melted, remove spoon, bring mixture to the boiling point, and let boil rapidly, without stirring, until mixture will form a jelly-like ball when tried in cold water.

Pour into bowl, set in pan of cold water, and, as mixture begins to cool, stir from sides of bowl, and, when cooled throughout, beat until white and creamy. Turn on a platter and knead until smooth. Put in bowl, cover with oiled paper to exclude air, that a crust may not form, and let stand twenty-four hours to ripen. Flavor with vanilla, shape into balls, and dip same as Chocolate Creams I. The mixture from which the centres are made is known as fondant, and constitutes the foundation of French candies.

CHOCOLATE CONES

Make fondant same as for Chocolate Creams II. To one-third the quantity add melted Walter Baker & Co.'s Premium No. 1 Chocolate and a few drops vanilla, working in with the hands. Shape into small cones and drop on an oiled paper or marble slab. Melt remaining fondant, flavor with vanilla or essence of violet, and color a light lavender, using a violet coloring. Dip cones, separately, and remove to oiled paper. As soon as set, dip bottom of each cone in melted Walter Baker & Co.'s Dot Chocolate, and roll chocolate portion, while still warm, in finely-chopped blanched Jordan almonds. White fondant may be used for the dipping; in which case, roll chocolate-covered portion in chopped Pistachio nuts.

CHOCOLATE CANDY

2 tablespoons butter,	2 cups sugar,
1 cup molasses,	1 cup milk,

½ lb. Walter Baker & Co.'s Premium No. 1 Chocolate.

Melt butter in granite-ware saucepan or iron kettle, and add molasses, sugar and milk; stir until sugar is dissolved, and, when boiling point is reached, add chocolate (melted over hot water) gradually, while stirring constantly. Let boil until, when tried in cold water, a firm ball may be formed between the fingers. Turn into a buttered pan, cool, and mark in small squares.

HUNTINGTON CHOCOLATE PUDDING

¼ cup butter,	3 teaspoons baking powder,
1 cup sugar,	Whites 2 eggs,
Yolks 2 eggs,	1½ squares Walter Baker & Co.'s
½ cup milk,	Premium No. 1 Chocolate,
1⅜ cups flour,	⅛ teaspoon salt,
	½ teaspoon vanilla.

Cream butter and add gradually, while beating constantly, one-half the sugar. Beat yolks of eggs until thick and lemon-colored, and add gradually, while beating constantly, remaining sugar. Combine mixtures and add milk alternately with flour mixed and sifted with baking powder and salt; then add whites of eggs beaten until stiff, chocolate (which has been melted over hot water) and vanilla. Turn into a buttered and floured angel-cake pan and bake in a moderate oven forty-five minutes.

Remove from pan to a serving dish, cool slightly, fill centre with whipped cream sweetened and flavored with vanilla and pour around.

CHOCOLATE SAUCE

Boil one cup sugar, one-half cup water and a few grains cream-of-tartar seven minutes. Melt one and one-half squares Walter Baker & Co.'s Premium No. 1 Chocolate and pour on gradually, while stirring constantly, the hot syrup. Flavor with one-fourth teaspoon vanilla.

BERKSHIRE CORNSTARCH PUDDING
(Without Eggs)

2 squares Walter Baker & Co.'s	3 tablespoons cornstarch,
Premium No. 1 Chocolate,	¾ cup milk,
2 cups milk,	¼ teaspoon salt,
¼ cup sugar,	½ teaspoon vanilla.

Put chocolate and two cups milk in double-boiler and cook until milk has scalded and chocolate has melted, stirring occasionally. Mix sugar, cornstarch and salt, add remaining milk and stir until thoroughly blended. Add cornstarch mixture gradually to chocolate mixture and cook ten minutes, stirring constantly until mixture thickens and afterwards occasionally. Turn into a serving dish and chill. Serve with or without sugar and cream.

FROZEN CHOCOLATE

1 quart milk,	1¼ cups sugar,
2½ squares Walter Baker & Co.'s	1 tablespoon vanilla,
Premium No. 1 Chocolate,	Few grains salt.

Put milk and chocolate in double-boiler and when milk has scalded and chocolate has melted add sugar, vanilla and salt. Chill and freeze, using three parts finely crushed ice to one part rock salt.

Serve in coupe glasses and garnish tops with whipped cream, sweetened and flavored with vanilla.

CHOCOLATE WALNUT WAFERS

½ cup butter,	1 cup chopped English Walnut meats,
1 cup sugar,	¼ teaspoon vanilla,
2 eggs,	⅛ teaspoon salt,
2 squares Walter Baker & Co.'s	⅔ cup bread flour.
Premium No. 1 Chocolate,	

Cream butter, and add sugar gradually, while beating constantly; then add eggs, well beaten, chocolate (which has been melted over hot water) nut meats, vanilla, salt and flour. Drop from tip of spoon, on a buttered tin sheet and bake in a moderate oven fifteen minutes.

NUT CHOCOLATE BARS

Whites 3 eggs,	1½ squares Walter Baker & Co.'s
7 ozs. powdered sugar,	Premium No. 1 Chocolate,
¼ lb. Jordan Almonds.	

Beat whites of eggs until stiff and add gradually, while beating constantly, powdered sugar. Fold in chocolate (which has been melted over hot water, then cooled slightly) and three-fourths of the almonds, blanched and chopped. Spread to one-fourth inch in thickness in a buttered dripping pan, sprinkle with remaining chopped nut meats and bake in a very slow oven forty-five minutes. Cut in finger-shaped pieces and remove from pan. Pile log cabin fashion on a fancy plate.

WELLESLEY LOAF CAKE

¼ cup butter,	2½ teaspoons baking powder,
1 cup sugar,	Whites 2 eggs,
Yolks 2 eggs,	2 squares Walter Baker & Co.'s
½ cup milk,	Premium No. 1 Chocolate,
1¼ cups flour,	½ teaspoon vanilla.

Cream butter and add sugar gradually, while beating constantly; then add yolks of eggs beaten until thick, milk, and flour mixed and sifted with baking powder. Add whites of eggs, beaten until stiff, chocolate (melted over hot water) and vanilla. Turn into a buttered and floured shallow cake pan, and bake in a moderate oven from thirty-five to forty minutes. Remove from pan, cover top with Wellesley frosting and when frosting is set pour over, a little at a time, two squares Walter Baker & Co.'s Premium No. 1 Chocolate (which has been melted over hot water) and spread evenly, using the back of a spoon.

WELLESLEY FROSTING

2 cups sugar,
½ cup boiling water,

Whites 2 eggs;
½ teaspoon vanilla.

Put sugar and water in saucepan, stir until sugar has dissolved. Bring to boiling point and let boil vigorously, without stirring, until syrup will thread when dropped from top of spoon. Put whites of eggs in saucepan and beat until stiff. Pour on the syrup gradually, while beating constantly, and continue the beating, until mixture is nearly stiff enough to spread. Place saucepan containing mixture in a larger saucepan, containing a small quantity of boiling water, place on range and cook, stirring constantly (scraping from bottom and sides of pan) until mixture becomes granular around sides of pan. Remove from saucepan of hot water, and beat until mixture will hold its shape; then add vanilla. Pour on cake and spread evenly, using a knife.

This is one of the varieties of thick, soft frostings which has recently met with so much favor.

FUDGE CAKE

1 cup butter,
1 cup sugar,
Yolks 3 eggs,
½ cup milk,
2 cups flour,

2½ teaspoons baking powder,
Whites 3 eggs,
2 ounces Walter Baker & Co.'s
Premium No. 1 Chocolate,
½ teaspoon vanilla.

Cream butter, add sugar gradually, while beating constantly, then add yolks of eggs well beaten. Mix and sift baking powder and flour, and add alternately with milk to the first mixture. Add whites of eggs beaten until stiff, chocolate melted over hot water, and vanilla.

Turn into two buttered and floured seven-inch square pans and bake in a moderate oven. Put between and on top Fudge Frosting.

Melt over hot water two ounces of Walter Baker & Co.'s Premium No. 1 Chocolate. Add gradually one-third cup butter, bit by bit, and stir until butter is melted, then add gradually, while beating constantly, one cup milk. Bring to the boiling point and add two cups sugar and let boil until mixture will form a very soft ball when tried in cold water ; the time required being about twenty minutes. Cool slightly, add one-half teaspoon flour and beat until of the right consistency to spread. One-fourth cup Jordan almonds, blanched and cut in pieces, may be added.

22

MISS FARMER'S CHOCOLATE NOUGAT CAKE

¼ a cup of butter,	3 teaspoonfuls of baking powder,
1½ cups of powdered sugar,	½ teaspoonful of vanilla,
1 egg,	2 squares of chocolate, melted,
1 cup of milk,	⅓ a cup of powdered sugar,
2 cups of bread flour,	⅔ a cup almonds blanched and shredded.

Cream the butter, add gradually one and one-half cups of sugar, and egg unbeaten; when well mixed, add two-thirds milk, flour mixed and sifted with baking powder, and vanilla. To melted chocolate add one-third a cup of powdered sugar, place on range, add gradually remaining milk, and cook until smooth. Cool slightly and add to cake mixture. Bake fifteen to twenty minutes in round layer-cake pans. Put between layers and on top of cake White Mountain Cream sprinkled with almonds.—*From Boston Cooking School Cook Book—Fannie Merritt Farmer.*

MISS FARMER'S CHOCOLATE CREAM CANDY

2 cups of sugar,	1 tablespoonful of butter,
⅔ a cup of milk,	2 squares of chocolate,
1 teaspoonful of vanilla.	

Put butter into granite saucepan; when melted add sugar and milk. Heat to boiling point; then add chocolate, and stir constantly until chocolate is melted. Boil thirteen minutes, remove from fire, add vanilla, and beat until creamy and mixture begins to sugar slightly around edge of saucepan. Pour at once into a buttered pan, cool slightly and mark in squares. Omit vanilla, and add, while cooking, one-fourth of a teaspoonful of cinnamon.—*Boston Cooking School Cook Book—Fannie Merritt Farmer.*

CHOCOLATE DOUGHNUTS

¼ cup butter,	1 cup sour milk,
1¼ cups sugar,	4 cups flour,
2 eggs,	1 teaspoonful soda,
1½ squares Walter Baker & Co.'s	1 teaspoonful cinnamon,
Premium No. 1 Chocolate,	¼ teaspoonful salt,
1¼ teaspoonfuls vanilla.	

Cream butter and add sugar gradually, while beating constantly; then add eggs well beaten, chocolate, melted, sour milk and flour mixed and sifted with soda, cinnamon and salt. Add vanilla and more flour, if necessary, to handle the mixture. Toss on a slightly floured board, knead slightly, and pat and roll to one-fourth inch in thickness. Shape with a doughnut cutter, first dipped in flour, fry in deep fat and drain on brown paper.

CHOCOLATE BREAD PUDDING

2 cups stale bread crumbs,	2 squares Walter Baker & Co.'s
1 quart scalded milk,	Premium No. 1 Chocolate,
Yolks 3 eggs,	¼ teaspoonful soda,
¼ cup sugar,	1 teaspoonful hot water,
Whites 3 eggs,	¼ teaspoonful salt.

Pour milk over bread crumbs, cover, and let stand **twenty minutes.** Add yolks of eggs, well beaten, mixed with sugar, melted chocolate, soda dissolved in water and salt; then fold in whites of eggs, beaten until stiff. Turn into a buttered pudding dish, and bake in a moderate oven fifty minutes. Serve with

FOAMY SAUCE

Yolk 1 egg,	⅛ teaspoonful salt,
1 cup powdered sugar,	½ teaspoonful vanilla,
½ cup scalded milk,	1 tablespoonful lemon juice,
1 teaspoonful cornstarch,	White 1 egg.

Beat egg yolk until thick, and add gradually, while beating constantly, three-fourths of the sugar. Mix remaining sugar with cornstarch and salt, and pour on gradually the scalded milk. Cook in double-boiler, ten minutes, stirring constantly until mixture thickens, then occasionally. Combine mixtures and add flavoring and egg white, beaten until stiff.

CHOCOLATE PUDDING
Marshmallow Mint Sauce

1 quart milk,	¼ teaspoonful salt,
1½ squares Walter Baker & Co.'s	2 tablespoonfuls granulated gelatine,
Premium No. 1 Chocolate,	3 tablespoonfuls cold water,
	⅓ cup sugar.

Put milk and chocolate in double-boiler, and when milk has scalded and chocolate melted, beat until smooth, using a wire whisk; then add sugar, salt, and gelatine, which has soaked in cold water ten minutes. As soon as gelatine has dissolved, strain and turn into a mould first dipped in cold water. Chill, remove from mould and pour around.

MARSHMALLOW MINT SAUCE

½ cup sugar,	White 1 egg,
¼ cup water,	1 drop oil of peppermint,
8 marshmallows,	Green coloring.

Boil sugar and water to a thin syrup (not thick enough to spin a thread) and add marshmallows cut in small pieces. Let stand two minutes, pressing marshmallows under syrup, using back of spoon. Pour mixture gradually while beating constantly on white of one egg, beaten until stiff, but not dry, and continue the beating until mixture is cool; then add oil of peppermint and color green.

CHOCOLATE
CARAMEL WALNUTS.
(See Page 39.)

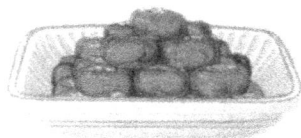

CHOCOLATE MARSHMALLOWS.
(See Page 50.)

FUDGE HEARTS OR ROUNDS
(See Page 44.)

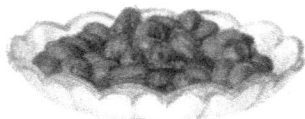

CHOCOLATE PEANUT CLUSTERS.
(See Page 41.)

BAKER'S CHOCOLATE "DIVINITY"
(See Page 46.)

CHOCOLATE PEPPERMINTS.
(See Page 49.)

CHOCOLATE OYSTERETTES.
(See Page 42.)

CHOCOLATE
DIPPED PEPPERMINTS
(See Page 40.)

WELLESLEY MARSHMALLOW FUDGE.
(See Page 43.)

PLAIN CHOCOLATE CARAMELS.
(See Page 47.)

COCOA FUDGE.
(See Page 32.)

MARSHMALLOW FUDGE.
(See Page 44.)

MAPLE FONDANT ACORNS.
(See Page 50.)

SURPRISE CHOCOLATE CREAMS
(See Page 54.)

NUT CHOCOLATE DROP COOKIES

½ cup butter,
1 cup sugar,
2 eggs,
2 squares Walter Baker & Co.'s
Premium No. 1 Chocolate,

1 cup chopped walnut meats,
¼ teaspoonful salt,
¼ teaspoonful vanilla,
⅔ cup flour.

Cream butter, and add sugar gradually, while beating constantly; then add eggs, well beaten, chocolate, melted, nut meats, salt, vanilla and flour. Drop from tip of spoon on a buttered sheet, one inch apart, and bake in a moderate oven.

CREOLE CAKE

½ cup butter,
2 cups brown sugar,
Yolks 3 eggs,
⅓ cup Baker's Breakfast Cocoa,

½ cup hot strong coffee infusion,
1 teaspoonful soda,
½ cup sour heavy cream,
2 cups flour,

Whites 3 eggs.

Cream butter and add sugar, gradually, while beating constantly; then add yolks of eggs beaten until thick. Add coffee infusion gradually to cocoa and let stand until cool. Add to first mixture, then add soda dissolved in cream, flour, and whites of eggs, beaten until stiff. Bake in layer cake tins in a moderate oven. Put layers together with boiled frosting, cover top with frosting and when set spread with a thin layer of Walter Baker & Co.'s Premium No. 1 Chocolate, melted.

BOILED FROSTING

1 cup sugar,
½ cup water,

Unbeaten white 1 egg,
½ teaspoonful vanilla.

Put sugar and water in saucepan, bring to the boiling point, and let boil vigorously, without stirring, until syrup will spin a thread when dropped from tip of spoon. Pour syrup gradually, while beating constantly (using an egg beater), on white of egg. Remove egg beater and continue the beating (using a spoon) until of the right consistency to spread; then add vanilla.

CHOCOLATE CREAM PEPPERMINTS

2 tablespoonfuls hot top milk,
½ tablespoonful melted butter,

3 drops oil of peppermint,
Confectioners' sugar,

"Dot" Chocolate.

Put top milk, melted butter and oil of peppermint in bowl. Add gradually, while beating constantly, confectioners' sugar, until mixture is stiff enough to knead, the amount required being about two cups. Work until creamy, using the hands. Shape in forty balls and flatten. Let stand until a crust is formed over the top. Dip one at a time in melted "Dot" Chocolate, and remove to paraffine paper.

25

CHOCOLATE DIPPED CANDIED ORANGE PEEL

Remove peel from four thin-skinned oranges in quarters. Cover with cold water, bring to the boiling point and let simmer until soft. Drain and cut in thin strips lengthwise, using scissors. Boil one cup sugar and one-half cup water, until syrup will spin a thread when dropped from tip of spoon. Add one-half the prepared strips, and press under syrup, using the back of spoon. Cook slowly six minutes, and remove to platter, using a fork, taking up as little syrup as possible. Cook remaining half in same manner. Let stand to dry off, then dip, one piece at a time, in melted "Dot" Chocolate, using the fingers. Remove to paraffine paper, and let stand until cool.

MISS M. E. ROBINSON'S RECIPES

PLAIN CHOCOLATE

1 ounce or square of Baker's Premium No. 1 Chocolate,
3 tablespoonfuls of sugar,   1 pint of boiling water,
⅛ a teaspoonful of salt,   1 pint of milk.

Place the chocolate, sugar and salt in the agate chocolate-pot or saucepan, add the boiling water and boil three minutes, stirring once or twice, as the chocolate is not grated. Add the milk and allow it time to heat, being careful not to boil the milk, and keep it closely covered, as this prevents the scum from forming. When ready to serve turn in chocolate-pitcher and beat with Dover egg-beater until light and foamy.

MOCHA JUMBLES

3 tablespoonfuls of butter,   1½ oz. of Premium Chocolate melted
1 cup of sugar,   in 1 tablespoonful of butter,
1 egg,   1½ to 2 cups of flour,
2 tablespoonfuls of cold coffee.   2 teaspoonfuls of baking powder,
                    ¼ teaspoonful of cinnamon.

Mix in order given, roll ⅓ inch in thickness, cut with doughnut cutter—sprinkle with sugar and bake.

STEAMED CHOCOLATE PUDDING

1 tablespoonful of butter,   ½ cup of sugar,
1½ oz. of Baker's Premium No. 1 Chocolate, ½ cup of milk,
1½ cups of flour,   2 teaspoonfuls of baking powder,
                    ½ teaspoonful of salt.

Steam one hour, serve with a hot, creamy sauce.

RECIPES
SPECIALLY PREPARED BY
MISS ELIZABETH KEVILL BURR

(All measurements should be level.)

FORMULA FOR MAKING THREE GALLONS OF BREAKFAST COCOA

½ a pound of Walter Baker & Co.'s Breakfast Cocoa,
1½ gallons of water, hot,   1½ gallons of milk, hot.

This should not be allowed to boil. Either make it in a large double-boiler, or a large saucepan or kettle over water. Mix the cocoa with enough cold water to make a paste, and be sure it is free from lumps. Heat together the milk and water, and pour in the cocoa ; then cook at least an hour, stirring occasionally.

CRACKED COCOA

To one-third a cup of Baker's Cracked Cocoa (sometimes called ''Cocoa Nibs'') use three cups of cold water; cook slowly at least one hour—the longer the better. Then strain the liquid and add one cup (or more if desired) of milk, and serve very hot. Do not allow the mixture to boil after milk has been added.

VANILLA CHOCOLATE WITH WHIPPED CREAM

One cake (½ a pound) of Walter Baker & Co.'s Vanilla Sweet Chocolate,
4 cups of boiling water,   Pinch of salt,   4 cups of hot milk.

This must be made in a double-boiler. Put the chocolate, boiling water and salt in upper part of the double-boiler. Stir and beat with a wooden spoon until the chocolate is dissolved and smooth. Add the milk and when thoroughly hot, strain, and serve with unsweetened whipped cream. More cooking will improve it.

CHOCOLATE CREAM PIE

Line a pie plate with rich pie crust, putting on an extra edge of crust the same as for custard pie. Fill with the chocolate filling made after the following recipe. Bake in a hot oven until crust is done ; remove, and when cool, cover with a meringue and brown very slowly in moderate oven.

CHOCOLATE FILLING

1 cup of milk,	2 level teaspoonfuls of flour,
Pinch of salt,	2 eggs (yolks),
1½ squares Baker's Premium No. 1	5 tablespoonfuls of sugar (level),
Chocolate,	1 teaspoonful of vanilla.

Put milk, salt and chocolate in upper part of the double-boiler, and when hot and smooth, stir in the flour, which has been mixed with enough cold milk to be thin enough to pour into the hot milk. Cook, stirring constantly, until it thickens; then let it cook eight or ten minutes. Mix the eggs and sugar together and pour the hot mixture over them, stirring well; put back in double-boiler and cook, stirring constantly, one minute. Remove, and when cool add one teaspoonful of vanilla.

MERINGUE

2 eggs (whites),	4 level tablespoonfuls of sugar,
Pinch of salt,	1 teaspoonful of vanilla.

Add salt to eggs and beat in a large, shallow dish with fork or egg-whip until stiff and flaky and dish can be turned upside down. Beat in the sugar slowly, then the vanilla, and beat until the dish can be turned upside down.

CHOCOLATE LAYER CAKE

5 level tablespoonfuls of butter,	About 2½ cups sifted flour,
3½ squares Baker's Premium No. 1	1 cup granulated sugar,
Chocolate (melted),	3 eggs,
1 cup milk,	3½ level teaspoonfuls baking
	powder.

Cream butter, add sugar, the melted chocolate, the whole eggs and beat all until smooth. Set this aside to cool. Add vanilla and half cup of the flour in which has been sifted the baking powder. Then add milk and remaining flour alternately, using enough flour to make mixture stiff enough to drop from the spoon. This may seem stiffer than other cake mixtures, but the amount of flour given will not be too much. Beat until very smooth.

Bake in square or round pans 20 or 25 minutes or until the cake springs back when pressed with the finger.

Put layers together with a thick, white frosting, lightly covered with marshmallows cut in small pieces, or omit the marshmallows and press half walnuts into the frosting, while it is soft. When the marshmallows are not used add 1 teaspoonful of vanilla to the cake mixture.

CHOCOLATE PARFAIT

1 qt. of heavy cream,   3 squares of Baker's Premium
1 cup of sugar,   No. 1 Chocolate,
2 teaspoonfuls of vanilla.

Put into the upper part of a double-boiler half cup of milk; when hot add chocolate and mix until chocolate has melted, then add sugar. Set this in pan of cold water, and as it cools add the cream slowly at first until mixture is smooth. Add vanilla and enough sugar to make quite sweet. Beat mixture until as stiff as for Charlotte Russe. Turn into a large mould, pack in ice and salt and let it stand at least two hours.

CHOCOLATE ALMONDS

Blanch the almonds by pouring boiling water on them, and let them stand two or three minutes. Roast them in oven. Dip them in the following recipe for chocolate coating, and drop on paraffine paper.

½ pound cake of Walter Baker's Vanilla Sweet Chocolate,
2 level tablespoonfuls of butter,   2 tablespoonfuls of boiling water.

Put chocolate in small saucepan over boiling water and when melted stir in butter and water. Mix well. If found to be too thick, add more water; if too thin, more chocolate.

HOT CHOCOLATE SAUCE

1 cup of boiling water,   1 square of chocolate,
Pinch of salt,   ½ a cup of sugar.

Cook all together slowly until it is the consistency of maple syrup, or thicker if desired. Just before serving, add one teaspoonful of vanilla. This will keep indefinitely, and can be reheated.

CHOCOLATE FROSTING

1 square of Baker's Premium   5 tablespoonfuls of boiling water,
No. 1 Chocolate,   1 teaspoonful of vanilla,
Pinch of salt,   About 3 cups of sifted confectioner's sugar.

Melt chocolate in bowl over tea-kettle, add water, salt and vanilla, and when smooth add the sugar, and beat until very glossy. Make the frosting stiff enough to spread without using a wet knife. It will keep indefinitely.

CHOCOLATE CAKE, OR DEVIL'S FOOD

5 level tablespoonfuls of butter,   1 teaspoonful of vanilla,
1¼ cups of sugar,   ¾ a cup of milk,
3½ squares of Baker's Premium   3½ level teaspoonfuls of baking powder,
No. 1 Chocolate, melted,   3 eggs,
1½ cups of sifted pastry flour.

Cream the butter, add sugar and chocolate, then the un-beaten eggs and vanilla, and beat together until very smooth. Sift the baking powder with one-half a cup of the flour, and use first; then alternate the milk and the remaining flour, and make the mixture stiff enough to drop from the spoon. Beat until very smooth and bake in loaf in moderate oven.

CHOCOLATE ICE-CREAM

1 quart of milk,	3 level tablespoonfuls of flour, ˙
Pinch of salt,	1 can sweetened condensed milk,
3 squares of Baker's Premium No. 1	3 eggs,
Chocolate,	6 level tablespoonfuls of sugar,
3 teaspoonfuls of vanilla.	

Put milk, salt and chocolate in double-boiler, and when milk is hot and chocolate has melted, stir in the flour, previously mixed in a little cold milk. Cook ten minutes, then pour this over the condensed milk, eggs and sugar mixed together; cook again for four minutes, stirring. Strain, and when cool add vanilla, and freeze.

CHOCOLATE WHIP

1 cup of milk,	2 eggs (yolks),
1½ squares of Baker's Premium No. 1 Chocolate,	6 level tablespoonfuls of sugar,
Pinch of salt,	2 teaspoonfuls of vanilla,
2 level tablespoonfuls of cornstarch,	5 eggs (whites).

Put milk, chocolate and salt in double-boiler; mix corn-starch in a small quantity of cold milk, and stir into the hot milk when the chocolate has been melted; stir until smooth, then cook twelve minutes. Mix together the yolks of the eggs and sugar, then pour the hot mixture over it; cook again one or two minutes, stirring. When very cold, just before serving, add the vanilla and fold in the stiffly beaten whites of the eggs. Pile lightly in a glass dish and serve with lady fingers. A meringue can be made of the whites of the eggs and sugar, then folded in the chocolate mixture, but it does not stand as long.

CHOCOLATE JELLY

1 pint of boiling water,	⅓ a package of gelatine,
2 pinches of salt,	2 level tablespoonfuls of sugar,
1½ squares Baker's Premium No. 1	1 teaspoonful of vanilla.
Chocolate,	

Put the water, salt and chocolate in a saucepan. Cook, stirring until the chocolate melts, then let it boil for three or five minutes. Soften the gelatine in a little cold water and pour the boiling mixture over it. Stir until dissolved, then add sugar and vanilla. Pour into a mould and set aside to harden, serve with cream and powdered sugar or sweetened whipped cream.

COTTAGE PUDDING

4 level tablespoonfuls of butter, 2 eggs,
1 cup of sugar, ¾ a cup of milk.

Two level teaspoonfuls of baking powder, one and three-quarters cups of sifted flour or enough to make mixture stiff enough to drop from the spoon. Bake in buttered gem pans in moderately hot oven twenty-three or twenty-five minutes. If the cake springs back after pressing a finger on the top, it shows that it is baked enough. To make a cocoa cottage pudding add to the above rule six level tablespoonfuls of cocoa. Serve with a vanilla sauce.

VANILLA SAUCE

2 level tablespoonfuls of butter, 1 cup of boiling water,
2 level tablespoonfuls of flour, 4 level tablespoonfuls of sugar,
Pinch of salt, 1 teaspoonful of vanilla.

Melt butter in saucepan, add flour and salt and mix until smooth; add slowly the boiling water, stirring and beating well. Add sugar and milk.

COCOANUT SOUFFLÉ

1 cup of milk, 4 level tablespoonfuls of sugar,
1 pinch of salt, Yolks of four eggs,
3 level tablespoonfuls of flour, 1 teaspoonful of vanilla,
  softened in a little cold milk, 1 cup of shredded cocoanut,
2 level tablespoonfuls of butter, Whites of four eggs.

Heat milk, add salt and flour and cook ten minutes after it has thickened. Mix together, butter, sugar and yolks of eggs. Pour hot mixture over, stirring well and set aside to cool. Add vanilla and cocoanut. Lastly fold in the stiffly beaten whites of the eggs. Bake in buttered pan, in moderate oven until firm. Serve hot with Chocolate Sauce.

CHOCOLATE SAUCE

2 level tablespoonfuls of butter, 1 square of Baker's Premium
1 level tablespoonful of flour, No. 1 Chocolate,
Pinch of salt, 4 level tablespoonfuls of sugar,
1 cup of boiling water, 1 teaspoonful of vanilla.

Melt butter in a saucepan, add dry flour and salt and mix until smooth, then add slowly the hot water, beating well. Add the square of chocolate and sugar and stir until melted. Add vanilla, just before serving.

COCOA BISCUIT

2 cups or 1 pint of sifted flour, 2 level tablespoonfuls of butter
3 level teaspoonfuls of baking powder, or lard,
½ a teaspoonful of salt, ⅔ a cup of milk or enough to
2 level tablespoonfuls of sugar, make a firm but not a stiff
4 level tablespoonfuls of Baker's Breakfast Cocoa. dough.

Sift all the dry ingredients together, rub in the butter with tips of the fingers. Stir in the required amount of milk. Turn out on slightly floured board, roll or pat out the desired thickness, place close together in pan and bake in very hot oven ten or fifteen minutes.

COCOA FUDGE

¼ a cup of milk,	6 tablespoonfuls of Baker's Breakfast Cocoa,
3 level tablespoonfuls of butter,	Pinch of salt,
2½ cups of powdered sugar,	1 teaspoonful of vanilla.

Mix all ingredients together but vanilla; cook, stirring constantly, until it begins to boil, then cook slowly, stirring occasionally, eight or ten minutes, or until it makes a firm ball when dropped in cold water. When cooked enough, add the vanilla and beat until it seems like very cold molasses in winter. Pour into a buttered pan; when firm, cut in squares. Great care must be taken not to beat too much, because it cannot be poured into the pan, and will not have a gloss on top.

MRS. RORER'S CHOCOLATE CAKE

2 ounces of chocolate,	½ a cup of butter,
4 eggs,	1½ cups of sugar,
½ a cup of milk,	1¾ cups of flour,
1 teaspoonful of vanilla,	1 heaping teaspoonful of baking powder.

Dissolve the chocolate in five tablespoonfuls of boiling water. Beat the butter to a cream, add the yolks, beat again, then the milk, then the melted chocolate and flour. Give the whole a vigorous beating. Now beat the whites of the eggs to a stiff froth, and stir them carefully into the mixture; add the vanilla and baking powder. Mix quickly and lightly, turn into well-greased cake pan and bake in a moderate oven forty-five minutes.—*From Mrs. Rorer's Cook Book.*

MRS. LINCOLN'S CHOCOLATE CARAMELS

One cup of molasses, half a cup of sugar, one-quarter of a pound of chocolate cut fine, half a cup of milk, and one heaping tablespoonful of butter. Boil all together, stirring all the time. When it hardens in cold water, pour it into shallow pans, and as it cools cut in small squares.—*From Mrs. Lincoln's Boston Cook Book.*

MRS. ARMSTRONG'S CHOCOLATE PUDDING

Soften three cups of stale bread in an equal quantity of milk. Melt two squares of Walter Baker & Co.'s Premium No. 1 Chocolate over hot water and mix with half a cup of sugar, a little salt, three beaten eggs and a half teaspoonful of vanilla. Mix this thoroughly with the bread and place in well-buttered custard cups. Steam about half an hour (according to size) and serve in the cups or turned out on warm plate.—*Mrs. Helen Armstrong.*

WALTER BAKER & CO.'S
GERMAN'S
SWEET CHOCOLATE

FAC-SIMILE ¼ LB. PACKAGE.

Walter Baker & Co's.
BREAKFAST
COCOA

FAC-SIMILE OF ½ LB. CAN.

WALTER BAKER & CO'S.
CARACAS SWEET CHOCOLATE

FAC-SIMILE 1/4 LB. PACKAGE

WALTER BAKER & CO.'S PREMIUM NO. 1 CHOCOLATE

FAC-SIMILE OF ½ LB. PACKAGE.

Walter Baker & Co's Premium No. 1 Chocolate

Has for more than 134 years held the highest place in the markets of the world solely by its unequaled quality. On account of its purity, delicacy of flavor, and that uniformity which insures the best results, it is the first choice of good housekeepers and cooks.

Beware of Imitations!

In view of the many imitations on the market, consumers should take care that they are supplied with the genuine article put up in the familiar blue carton and yellow label (note facsimile on the opposite page) bearing our trade-mark, La Belle Chocolatière, on the back.

MRS. ARMSTRONG'S CHOCOLATE CHARLOTTE

Soak a quarter of a package of gelatine in one-fourth of a cupful of cold water. Whip one pint of cream to a froth and put it in a bowl, which should be placed in a pan of ice-water. Put an ounce of Walter Baker & Co.'s Premium No. 1 Chocolate in a small pan with two tablespoonfuls of sugar and one of boiling water, and stir over the hot fire until smooth and glossy. Add to this a gill of hot milk and the soaked gelatine, and stir until the gelatine is dissolved. Sprinkle a generous half cupful of powdered sugar over the cream. Now add the chocolate and gelatine mixture and stir gently until it begins to thicken. Line a quart charlotte mould with lady fingers, and when the cream is so thick that it will just pour, turn it gently into the mould. Place the charlotte in a cold place for an hour or more, and at serving time turn out on a flat dish.—*Mrs. Helen Armstrong.*

CHOCOLATE JELLY WITH CRYSTALLIZED GREEN GAGES

Dissolve in a quart of water three tablespoonfuls of grated chocolate; let come to a boil; simmer ten minutes; add a cup of sugar and a box of gelatine (that has been softened in a cup of water) and strain through a jelly bag or two thicknesses of cheese-cloth. When almost cold, add a dessertspoonful of vanilla and a tablespoonful of brandy. Then whisk well; add half a pound of crystallized green gages cut into small pieces; pour into a pretty mould, and when cold serve with whipped cream.

MRS. HILL'S COCOA FRAPPÉ

Mix half a pound of cocoa and three cupfuls of sugar; cook with two cupfuls of boiling water until smooth; add to three quarts and a half of milk scalded with cinnamon bark; cook for ten minutes. Beat in the beaten whites of two eggs mixed with a cupful of sugar and a pint of whipped cream. Cool, flavor with vanilla extract, and freeze. Serve in cups. Garnish with whipped cream.—*Janet McKenzie Hill—Ladies' Home Journal.*

MRS. HILL'S CHOCOLATE PUFFS

Stir a cupful of flour into a cupful of water and half a cupful of butter, boiling together; remove from fire, beat in an ounce of melted chocolate, and, one at a time, three large eggs. Shape with forcing bag and rose tube. Bake, cut off the tops and put into each cake a tablespoonful of strawberry preserves. Cover with whipped cream sweetened and flavored.—*Janet McKenzie Hill—Ladies' Home Journal.*

34

MRS. BEDFORD'S CHOCOLATE CRULLERS

Cream two tablespoonfuls of butter and one-half of a cupful of sugar; gradually add the beaten yolks of three eggs and one and one-half cupfuls more of sugar, one cupful of sour milk, one teaspoonful of vanilla, two ounces of chocolate grated and melted over hot water, one-third of a teaspoonful of soda dissolved in one-half of a teaspoonful of boiling water, the whites of the eggs whipped to a stiff froth, and sufficient sifted flour to make a soft dough. Roll out, cut into oblongs; divide each into three strips, leaving the dough united at one end. Braid loosely, pinch the ends together and cook until golden-brown in smoking-hot fat. — *Mrs. Cornelia C. Bedford.*

MRS. BEDFORD'S HOT COCOA SAUCE FOR ICE-CREAM

Boil together one and one-half cupfuls of water and one cupful of sugar for two minutes; add one tablespoonful of arrowroot dissolved in a little cold water, stir for a moment, then boil until clear. Add two tablespoonfuls of cocoa which has been dissolved in a little hot water and a tiny pinch of salt and boil three minutes longer. Take from the fire and add one teaspoonful of vanilla. — *Mrs. Cornelia C. Bedford.*

MRS. BEDFORD'S CHOCOLATE MACAROONS

Grate one-quarter of a pound of chocolate and mix one-quarter of a pound of sifted powdered sugar and one-quarter of a pound of blanched and ground almonds. Add a pinch of cinnamon and mix to a soft paste with eggs beaten until thick. Drop in half-teaspoonfuls on slightly buttered paper and bake in a moderate oven. Do not take from the paper until cold; then brush the under side with cold water, and the paper can be readily stripped off. — *Mrs. Cornelia C. Bedford.*

MRS. EWING'S CREAMY COCOA

Stir together in a saucepan half a cup of Walter Baker & Co.'s Breakfast Cocoa, half a cup of flour, half a cup of granulated sugar and half a teaspoonful of salt. Add gradually one quart of boiling water and let the mixture boil five minutes, stirring it constantly. Remove from the fire, add a quart of boiling milk, and serve. If desired a spoonful of whipped cream may be put in each cup before filling with the cocoa.

The proportions given will make delicious, creamy cocoa, sufficient to serve twelve persons. The flour should be sifted before it is measured. — *By Mrs. Emma P. Ewing, author of "The Art of Cookery."*

35

MRS. EWING'S CREAMY CHOCOLATE

Mix together half a cup of sifted flour, half a cup of granulated sugar and half a teaspoonful of salt. Put into a saucepan half a cup of Walter Baker & Co.'s Premium No. 1 Chocolate, finely shaved. Add one quart of boiling water, stir until dissolved, add the flour, sugar and salt, and boil gently, stirring constantly, five minutes. Then stir in a quart of boiling milk, and serve with or without whipped cream.— *By Mrs. Emma P. Ewing, author of "The Art of Cookery."*

MRS. SALZBACHER'S CHOCOLATE HEARTS

Melt, by standing over hot water, three ounces of unsweetened chocolate; add a pound of sifted powdered sugar and mix thoroughly; work to a stiff yet pliable paste with the unbeaten whites of three eggs (or less), adding vanilla to flavor. If the paste seems too soft, add more sugar. Break off in small pieces and roll out about one-fourth of an inch thick, sprinkling the board and paste with granulated sugar instead of flour. Cut with a tiny heart-shaped cake cutter (any other small cake cutter will do), and place on pans oiled just enough to prevent sticking. Bake in a very moderate oven. When done, they will feel firm to the touch, a solid crust having formed over the top. They should be very light, and will loosen easily from the pan after being allowed to stand a moment to cool. The success of these cakes depends upon the oven, which should not be as cool as for meringue, nor quite so hot as for sponge cake. If properly made, they are very excellent and but little labor. Use the yolks for chocolate whips.— *From "Good Housekeeping."*

CHOCOLATE FUDGE WITH FRUIT

Two cups of sugar, one-half cup of milk, one-half cup of molasses, one-half cup of butter; mix all together and boil seven minutes; add one-half cup of Baker's Premium No. 1 Chocolate and boil seven minutes longer. Then add two tablespoonfuls of figs, two tablespoonfuls of raisins, one-half a cup of English walnuts and one teaspoonful of vanilla.

CHOCOLATE MACAROONS

Stir to a paste whites of seven eggs, three-fourths a pound of sifted sugar, one-half a pound of almonds pounded very fine, and two ounces of grated Baker's Premium No. 1 Chocolate. Have ready wafer paper cut round, on which lay pieces of the mixture rolled to fit the wafer. Press one-half a blanched almond on each macaroon and bake in a moderate oven.

COCOA CHARLOTTE
(Without Cream)

1 pint of water,   ½ a cup of sugar,
Whites of 2 eggs,   2 level tablespoonfuls of cornstarch,
½ a teaspoonful of vanilla, ½ a teaspoonful of cinnamon,
      3 tablespoonfuls of cocoa.

Dissolve the cornstarch in a quarter of a cup of cold water, add it to the pint of boiling water, stir until it thickens, add the sugar and the cocoa, which have been thoroughly mixed together. Remove from the fire, add the cinnamon and vanilla, and pour slowly over the stiffly beaten whites of eggs. Pour at once into a pudding mould, and put away in a cold place to harden. Serve with plain cream. — *Mabel Richards Dulon*.

PETITS FOUR

Bake a simple, light sponge cake in a shallow biscuit tin or dripping pan, and when cold turn out on the moulding board and cut into small dominoes or diamonds. They should be about an inch in depth. Split each one and spread jelly or frosting between the layers, then ice tops and sides with different tinted icings, pale green flavored with pistachio, pale pink with rose, yellow with orange, white with almond. Little domino cakes are also pretty. Ice the cakes on top and sides with white icing, then when hard put on a second layer of chocolate, using Baker's Premium No. 1 Chocolate, and made as for layer cake, dipping the brush in the melted chocolate to make the spots.

Candied violets, bits of citron cut in fancy shapes, candied cherries and angelica may all be utilized in making pretty designs in decoration.—*American Housekeeper*.

POTATO CAKE

Two cups of white sugar, one cup of butter, one cup of hot mashed potatoes, one cup of chopped walnuts, half a cup of sweet milk, two cups of flour, four eggs well beaten, five teaspoonfuls of melted chocolate, one tablespoonful each of cloves, cinnamon and nutmeg, two teaspoonfuls of baking powder. Bake in layers and use marshmallow filling.

SPANISH CHOCOLATE CAKE

One cup of sugar, one-half a cup of butter, one-half a cup of sweet milk, three cups of flour, two eggs, one teaspoonful of soda dissolved in hot water. Put on the stove one cup of milk, one-half a cup of Baker's Premium No. 1 Chocolate, grated; stir until dissolved; then stir into it one cup of sugar and the yolk of one egg stirred together; when cool flavor with vanilla. While this is cooling beat up the first part of the cake and add the chocolate custard. ·Bake in layers. Ice on top and between the layers.

CHOCOLATE JUMBLES

4 cups flour,	2 eggs,
1 cup washed butter,	1 teaspoonful soda,
1½ cups sugar,	¾ tablespoonful hot water.

Work butter into flour, using the tips of the fingers. Beat eggs until light and add sugar, gradually, continuing the beating. Combine mixtures and add soda dissolved in water. Mixture should now be of the right consistency to roll, but if a bit too stiff, add a small quantity of milk. Toss on a slightly floured board and pat and roll to one-eighth inch in thickness. Shape with a fancy cutter, first dipped in flour. Put on a buttered tin, and bake in a moderate oven. Cool and spread with

CHOCOLATE FROSTING

½ cake Walter Baker's	1 cup sugar,
Sweet Vanilla Chocolate,	1 teaspoonful butter,
½ cup of milk,	1 teaspoonful vanilla,
Few grains salt.	

Put chocolate in small saucepan, place in larger saucepan containing boiling water, and, when melted, add butter; then add milk and sugar alternately, stirring between the additions. When mixture is smooth, place in direct contact with range, bring to the boiling point, and let boil until mixture will just hold together when tried in cold water. Remove from range, cool slightly, beat until of the right consistency to spread, and add vanilla and salt.

TURKEY TROT

1 cup molasses,	Yolks 2 eggs,
½ cup sugar,	1 tablespoonful soda,
⅓ cup (grated) Walter Baker's	3 tablespoonfuls hot water,
Sweet Chocolate,	1 teaspoonful vanilla,
3 tablespoonfuls butter,	Flour.

Mix molasses, sugar and grated chocolate. Add butter, melted, yolks of eggs slightly beaten, soda dissolved in water and vanilla; then add enough flour to make of right consistency to roll. Chill, toss one-quarter at a time on a slightly floured board, pat and roll to one-eighth inch in thickness, and shape, with a tin cutter, in the form of a turkey, first dipped in flour. Put on a buttered tin and bake in a moderate oven. Ornament each with the words "Turkey Trot" made by forcing ornamental frosting, white or pink, through a pastry bag and tube.

SPECIALLY PREPARED BY
MRS. JANET McKENZIE HILL

PEPPERMINTS, CHOCOLATE MINTS, Etc.
(Uncooked Fondant)

White of 1 egg,
2 tablespoonfuls of cold water,
Sifted confectioner's sugar,
½ a teaspoonful of essence of peppermint or a few drops of oil of peppermint,

1 or 2 squares of Baker's Premium No. 1 Chocolate,
Green color paste,
Pink color paste.

Beat the egg on a plate, add the cold water and gradually work in sugar enough to make a firm paste. Divide the sugar paste into three parts. To one part add the peppermint and a very little of the green color paste. Take the paste from the jar with a wooden tooth pick, add but a little. Work and knead the mixture until the paste is evenly distributed throughout. Roll the candy into a sheet one-fourth of an inch thick, then cut out into small rounds or other shape with any utensil that is convenient. Color the second part a very delicate pink, flavor with rose extract and cut out in the same manner as the first. To the last part add one or two squares of Baker's Chocolate, melted over hot water, and flavor with peppermint. Add also a little water, as the chocolate will make the mixture thick and crumbly. Begin by adding a tablespoonful of water, then add more if necessary, knead and cut these as the others.

CHOCOLATE CARAMEL WALNUTS
(Uncooked Fondant)

White of 1 egg,
3 tablespoonfuls of maple or caramel syrup,
1 tablespoonful of water,
Sifted confectioner's sugar,

1 teaspoonful of vanilla extract,
2 or more squares of Baker's Premium No. 1 Chocolate,
English walnuts.

Beat the white of egg slightly, add the syrup, water, sugar as needed, the chocolate, melted over hot water, and the vanilla, also more water if necessary. Work with a silver-plated knife and knead until thoroughly mixed, then break off small pieces of uniform size and roll them into balls, in the hollow of the hand, flatten the balls a little, set the half of an English walnut upon each, pressing the nut into the candy and thus flattening it still more. The caramel gives the chocolate a particularly nice flavor.

HOW TO COAT CANDIES, &c.,
WITH BAKER'S "DOT" CHOCOLATE

Half a pound of "Dot" Chocolate will coat quite a number of candy or other "centers," but as depth of chocolate and an even temperature during the whole time one is at work are essential, it is well, when convenient, to melt a larger quantity of chocolate. When cold, the unused chocolate may be cut from the dish and set aside for use at a future time. If the chocolate be at the proper temperature when the centers are dipped in it, it will give a rich, glossy coating free from spots, and the candies will not have a spreading base. After a few centers have been dipped set them in a cool place to harden. The necessary utensils are a wire fork and a very small double boiler. The inner dish of the boiler should be of such size that the melted chocolate will come nearly to the top of it. Break the chocolate in small pieces and surround with warm water, stir occasionally while melting. When the melted chocolate has cooled to about 80° F. it is ready to use. Drop whatever is to be coated into the chocolate, with the fork push it below the chocolate, lift out, draw across the edge of the dish and drop onto a piece of table oil cloth or onto waxed paper. Do not let a drop of water get into the chocolate.

CHOCOLATE DIPPED PEPPERMINTS
(Uncooked Fondant)

Prepare green, white, pink and chocolate colored mints by the first recipe. After they have dried off a little run a spatula under each and turn to dry the other side. Coat with Baker's "Dot" Chocolate.

GINGER, CHERRY, APRICOT and NUT CHOCOLATES

White of 1 egg,	Candied cherries,
2 tablespoonfuls of cold water,	Candied apricots,
Sifted confectioner's sugar,	Halves of almonds,
Almond or rose extract,	Halves of pecan nuts,
Preserved ginger,	½ a pound of Baker's "Dot" Chocolate.

Use the first four ingredients in making uncooked fondant. (Caramel syrup is a great addition to this fondant, especially if nuts are to be used. Use three tablespoonfuls of syrup and one tablespoonful of water with one egg white instead of the two tablespoonfuls of water indicated in the recipe.) Work the fondant for some time, then break off little bits and wrap around small pieces of the fruit, then roll in the hollow of the hand into balls or oblongs. For other candies, roll a piece of the fondant into a ball, flatten it with the fingers and use to cover a whole pecan or English walnut meat. Set each shape on a plate as it is finished. They will harden very quickly. Dip these, one by one, in Baker's "Dot" Chocolate and set on an oil cloth.

PEPPERMINTS,
CHOCOLATE MINTS, ETC.
(See Page 39.)

CHOCOLATE DIPPED
PARISIAN SWEETS
(See Page 41.)

VASSAR FUDGE.
(See Page 43.)

GINGER, CHERRY, APRICOT
AND NUT CHOCOLATES.
(See Page 40)

CHOCOLATE COCOANUT CAKES.
(See Page 45.)

CHOCOLATE NUT CARAMELS.
(See Page 47.)

ALMOND AND CHERRY CHOCOLATE CREAMS.
(See Page 49.)

CHOCOLATE MOLASSES KISSES.
(See Page 55.)

CHOCOLATE PEANUT BRITTLE.
(See Page 54.)

CHOCOLATE COATED ALMONDS.
(See Page 41.)

STUFFED DATES,
CHOCOLATE DIPPED.
(See Page 41.)

CHOCOLATE DIPPED
FRUIT FUDGE.
(See Page 45.)

CHOCOLATE NOUGATINES.
(See Page 46.)

CHOCOLATE PEANUT CLUSTERS

Shell a quart of freshly-roasted peanuts and remove the skins. Drop the peanuts, one by one, into the centre of a dish of " Dot " Chocolate made ready for use; lift out onto oil cloth with a dipping fork (a wire fork comes for the purpose, but a silver oyster fork answers nicely) to make groups of three nuts,— two below, side by side, and one above and between the others.

CHOCOLATE COATED ALMONDS

Select nuts that are plump at the ends. Use them without blanching. Brush, to remove the dust. Melt "Dot" Chocolate and when cooled properly drop the nuts, one at a time, into the center of it; push the nuts under with the fork, then drop onto waxed paper or oil cloth. In removing the fork make a design on the top of each nut. These are easily prepared and are particularly good.

PLAIN AND CHOCOLATE DIPPED PARISIAN SWEETS

½ a cup of Sultana raisins,
5 figs,
1 cup of dates,
2 ounces of citron,
⅔ a cup of nut meats, (almonds, filberts, pecans or walnuts, one

variety or a mixture),
1½ ounces of Baker's Premium No. 1 Chocolate,
⅓ a cup of confectioner's sugar,
¼ a teaspoonful salt,
Chocolate Fondant or Baker's "Dot" Chocolate.

Pour boiling water over the figs and dates, let boil up once, then drain as dry as possible; remove stones from the dates, the stem ends from the figs; chop the fruit and nut meats (almonds should be blanched) in a food chopper; add the salt; and the sugar and work the whole to a smooth paste; add the chocolate, melted, and work it evenly through the mass. Add more sugar if it is needed and roll the mixture into a sheet one-fourth an inch thick. Cut into strips an inch wide. Cut the strips into diamond-shaped pieces (or squares); roll these in confectioner's sugar or dip them in chocolate fondant or in Baker's "Dot" Chocolate, and sprinkle a little fine-chopped pistachio nut meats on the top of the dipped pieces. When rolling the mixture use confectioner's sugar on board and rolling pin.

STUFFED DATES, CHOCOLATE DIPPED

Cut choice dates open on one side and remove the seeds. Fill the open space in the dates with a strip of preserved ginger or pineapple, chopped nuts or chopped nuts mixed with white or chocolate fondant; press the dates into a compact form to keep in the filling, then dip them, one by one, in "Dot" Chocolate.

CHOCOLATE OYSTERETTES,
PLAIN AND WITH CHOPPED FIGS

Oyster crackers, salted preferred,   fruit cut in very small bits,
Fine-chopped roasted peanuts, or raisins   ½ a pound or more of Baker's
   or 3 or 4 basket figs or a little French   "Dot" Chocolate.

Select fresh-baked crackers free from crumbs. Dip in "Dot" Chocolate, made ready as in previous recipes, and dispose on oil cloth or waxed paper. For a change add figs or other fruit, cut very fine, or chopped nuts to the chocolate ready for dipping.

TURKISH PASTE WITH FRENCH FRUIT,
CHOCOLATE FLAVORED

3 level tablespoonfuls of granulated   2 squares of Baker's Premium
   gelatine,   No. 1 Chocolate,
½ a cup of cold water,   1 teaspoonful of vanilla extract,
2 cups of sugar,   1 cup of French candied fruit
⅔ a cup of cold water,   (cherries, angelica, citron,
1 teaspoonful of ground cinnamon,   etc.), chopped fine.

Let the gelatine stand in the half cup of cold water until it has taken up all of the water. Stir the sugar and the two-thirds a cup of cold water over the fire until the sugar is dissolved and the syrup is boiling, then add the gelatine and let cook twenty minutes; add the cinnamon, the chocolate, melted over hot water, and beat all together, then add the vanilla and the fruit; let stand in a cool place for a time, then when it thickens a little turn into an *un*buttered bread pan and set aside until the next day. To unmould separate the paste from the pan—at the edge—with a sharp-pointed knife. Sift confectioner's sugar over the top, then with the tips of the fingers gently pull the paste from the pan to a board dredged with confectioner's sugar; cut into strips, then into small squares. Roll each square in confectioner's sugar. In cutting keep sugar between the knife and the paste.

CHOICE CHOCOLATE PECAN PRALINES

3 cups of granulated sugar,   2 squares of Baker's Premium
1 cup of cream,   No. 1 Chocolate,
1 cup of sugar cooked to caramel,   3 cups of pecan nut meats.

Stir the sugar and cream over the fire until the sugar is melted, then let boil to the soft ball degree, or to 236° F. Add the chocolate, melted or shaved fine, and beat it in, then pour the mixture onto the cup of sugar cooked to caramel; let the mixture boil up once, then remove from the fire; add the nut meats and beat until the mass begins to thicken. When cold enough to hold its shape drop onto an oil cloth or marble, a teaspoonful in a place, and at once set a half nut meat on each. Two persons are needed to make these pralines, one to drop the mixture, the other to decorate with the halves of the nuts. The mixture becomes smooth and firm almost instantly. Maple or brown sugar may be used in place of all or a part of the quantity of granulated sugar designated.

VASSAR FUDGE

2 cups of white granulated sugar,	1 cup of cream,
1 tablespoonful of butter,	¼ a cake of Baker's Premium No. 1 Chocolate.

Put in the sugar and cream, and when this becomes hot put in the chocolate, broken up into fine pieces. Stir vigorously and constantly. Put in butter when it begins to boil. Stir until it creams when beaten on a saucer. Then remove and beat until quite cool and pour into buttered tins. When cold cut in diamond-shaped pieces.

SMITH COLLEGE FUDGE

Melt one-quarter cup of butter. Mix together in a separate dish one cup of white sugar, one cup of brown sugar, one-quarter cup of molasses and one-half cup of cream. Add this to the butter, and after it has been brought to a boil continue boiling for two and one-half minutes, stirring rapidly. Then add two squares of Baker's Premium No. 1 Chocolate, scraped fine. Boil this five minutes, stirring it first rapidly, and then more slowly towards the end. After it has been taken from the fire, add one and one-half teaspoonfuls of vanilla. Then stir constantly until the mass thickens. Pour into buttered pan and set in a cool place.

WELLESLEY MARSHMALLOW FUDGE

Heat two cups of granulated sugar and one cup of rich milk (cream is better). Add two squares of Baker's Premium No. 1 Chocolate, and boil until it hardens in cold water. Just before it is done add a small piece of butter, then begin to stir in marshmallows, crushing and beating them with a spoon. Continue to stir in marshmallows, after the fudge has been taken from the fire, until half a pound has been stirred into the fudge. Cool in sheets three-quarters of an inch thick, and cut in cubes.

DOUBLE FUDGE

2 cups of granulated sugar,	2 squares of Baker's Premium No. 1 Chocolate,
½ a cup of cream,	1 tablespoonful of butter.

Boil seven minutes; then beat and spread in buttered tin to cool.

| 2 cups of brown sugar, | 1 teaspoonful of vanilla extract, |
| ½ a cup of cream, | 1 cup of walnut meats chopped fine, |

Butter size of a walnut.

Boil ten minutes ; then beat and pour on top of fudge already in pan. When cool, cut in squares.

MARBLED FUDGE

2 cups of granulated sugar,	2 squares of Baker's Premium
¼ a cup of glucose (pure corn syrup),	No. 1 Chocolate, scraped
1½ cups cream,	fine or melted,
1 tablespoonful of butter,	2 teaspoonfuls of vanilla.

Stir the sugar, glucose and cream over a slack fire until the sugar is melted ; move the saucepan to a hotter part of the range and continue stirring until the mixture boils, then let boil, stirring every three or four minutes very gently, until the thermometer registers 236° F., or till a soft ball can be formed in cold water. Remove from the fire and pour one-half of the mixture over the chocolate. Set both dishes on a cake rack, or on something that will allow the air to circulate below the dishes. When the mixture cools a little get someone to beat one dish of the fudge ; add a teaspoonful of vanilla to each dish, and beat until thick and slightly grainy, then put the mixture into a pan, lined with waxed paper, first a little of one and then of the other, to give a marbled effect. When nearly cold turn from the pan, peel off the paper and cut into cubes.

FUDGE HEARTS OR ROUNDS

2 cups of granulated sugar,	¼ a cup of butter,
⅔ a cup of condensed milk,	1½ squares of Baker's Premium
⅔ a cup of water,	No. 1 Chocolate,

1 teaspoonful of vanilla extract.

Boil the sugar, milk and water to 236° F., or to the "soft ball" degree ; stir gently every few minutes ; add the butter and let boil up vigorously, then remove from the fire and add the chocolate ; let stand undisturbed until cool, then add the vanilla and beat the candy until it thickens and begins to sugar. Pour into a pan lined with paper to stand until cooled somewhat ; turn from the mould and with a French cutter or a sharp edged tube cut into symmetrical shapes.

MARSHMALLOW FUDGE

1st BATCH	2nd BATCH
2 cups of granulated sugar,	2 cups of granulated sugar,
1 cup of cream,	1 cup of cream,
¾ a teaspoonful of salt,	¼ a teaspoonful of salt,
1 tablespoonful of butter,	1 tablespoonful of butter,
2 squares of Baker's Premium No. 1 Chocolate,	2 squares of Baker's Premium No. 1 Chocolate,
1 teaspoonful of vanilla,	1 teaspoonful of vanilla.
Nearly half a pound of marshmallows, split in halves.	

44

Start with the first batch and when this is nearly boiled enough, set the second batch to cook, preparing it in the same manner as the first. Stir the sugar and cream, over a rather slack fire, until the sugar is melted, when the sugar boils wash down the sides of the pan as in making fondant, set in the thermometer and cook over a quick fire, without stirring, to the soft ball degree, 236° F.; add the butter, salt and chocolate, melted or shaved fine, and let boil up vigorously, then remove to a cake cooler (or two spoon handles to allow a circulation of air below the pan). In the meantime the second batch should be cooking and the marshmallows be gotten ready. When the first batch is about cold add the vanilla and beat the candy vigorously until it begins to thicken, then turn it into a pan lined with waxed paper. At once dispose the halves of marshmallows close together upon the top of the fudge. Soon the other dish of fudge will be ready; set it into cold water and when nearly cold, add the vanilla and beat as in the first batch, then pour it over the marshmallows. When the whole is about cold turn it onto a marble, or hardwood board, pull off the paper and cut into cubes. If one is able to work very quickly, but one batch need be prepared, half of it being spread over the marshmallows.

CHOCOLATE DIPPED FRUIT FUDGE

FRUIT FUDGE
1½ cups of granulated sugar,
1 cup of maple syrup
1½ cups of glucose (pure corn syrup),
½ a cup of thick cream, or
⅓ a cup of milk and ¼ a cup of butter,

¾ a cup of fruit, figs, and candied cherries and apricots, cut in small pieces.
CHOCOLATE FOR DIPPING
½ a cake or more of Baker's "Dot" Chocolate.

Stir the sugar, syrup, glucose and cream until the sugar is melted, cover and let boil three or four minutes, then uncover and let boil, stirring often but very gently until a soft ball may be formed in cold water, or until the thermometer registers 236° F. Set the saucepan on a cake cooler and when the mixture becomes cool, add the fruit and beat until it becomes thick, then turn into pans lined with waxed paper. In about fifteen minutes cut into squares. Coat these with the " Dot" Chocolate.

CHOCOLATE COCOANUT CAKES

⅔ a cup of granulated sugar,
¼ a cup (scant measure) of water,
One cup, less one tablespoonful, of glucose,

½ a pound of dessicated cocoanut,
½ a pound of Baker's "Dot" Chocolate.

Heat the sugar, water and glucose to the boiling point, add the cocoanut and stir constantly while cooking to the soft ball degree, or until a little of the candy dropped on a cold marble may be rolled into a ball. Drop, by small teaspoonfuls, onto a marble or waxed paper, to make small, thick, rather uneven rounds. When cold coat with "Dot" Chocolate melted over hot water and cooled properly. These cakes are very easily coated.

BAKER'S CHOCOLATE "DIVINITY"

1½ cups of brown sugar,
1 cup of maple syrup,
½ a cup of glucose (pure corn syrup),
⅓ a cup of water,
¼ a teaspoonful of salt,
The whites of 2 eggs.
1 cup of nut meats, chopped fine,
2 squares of Baker's Premium No. 1 Chocolate, broken in pieces.

Let the sugar, syrup, glucose and water stand on the back of the range, stirring occasionally, until the sugar is melted, then cover and let boil five minutes. Remove the cover and let boil to soft crack, 287° F., or, until when tested in water a ball that rattles in the cup will be formed. Add the salt and chocolate and beat over the fire, until the chocolate is melted, then pour in a fine stream onto the whites of eggs, beaten dry, beating constantly meanwhile; add the nuts and pour into a pan lined with waxed paper. In about fifteen minutes lift the candy from the pan (by the ends of the paper left for the purpose) and cut it into small oblongs or squares. The candy must be stirred constantly during the last of the cooking. In cooking without a thermometer one is liable to remove the candy from the fire too soon — if this happens, return, egg whites and all, to the saucepan, set this into a dish of boiling water and stir constantly until the mixture thickens, then pour into the pan lined with paper. On no account let even a few drops of water boil into the candy.

CHOCOLATE NOUGATINES

1 cup of granulated sugar,
⅓ a cup of glucose,
⅓ a cup of honey (strained),
Piece of paraffine size of a pea,
¼ a cup of water,
¾ a teaspoonful of salt,
The whites of 2 eggs, beaten dry,
1 cup of almond or English walnut meats, chopped fine,
1 teaspoonful of vanilla,
About ½ a pound of Baker's "Dot" Chocolate.

Put the sugar, glucose, honey, paraffine and water over the fire, stir occasionally and let boil to the hard ball degree, about 248° F. Add the salt to the eggs, before beating them, and gradually pour on part of the syrup, beating constantly meanwhile with the egg beater; return the rest of the syrup to the fire and let boil until it is brittle when tested in cold water, or to 290° F. Then turn this gradually onto the eggs, beating constantly meanwhile. Return the whole to the saucepan, set over the fire on an asbestos mat and beat constantly until it becomes crisp when tested in cold water. Pour into a buttered pan a little larger than an ordinary bread pan and set aside to become cold. When cold cut into pieces about an inch and a quarter long and three-eighths of an inch wide and thick. Coat these with "Dot" Chocolate.

46

PLAIN CHOCOLATE CARAMELS

2½ cups of sugar,
¾ a cup of glucose (pure corn
   syrup),
½ a cup of butter,
⅛ a teaspoonful of cream of tartar,

2½ cups of whole milk
   (not skimmed),
2½ squares of Baker's Premium
   No. 1 Chocolate,
1 teaspoonful of vanilla extract.

Put the sugar, glucose, butter, cream of tartar and one cup of the milk over the fire, stir constantly, and when the mass has boiled a few moments, gradually stir in the rest of the milk. Do not let the mixture stop boiling while the milk is being added. Stir every few moments and cook to 248° F., or until, when tested in cold water, a hard ball may be formed; add the chocolate and vanilla and beat them thoroughly through the candy, then turn it into two bread pans. When nearly cold cut into squares.

CHOCOLATE NUT CARAMELS

2 cups of granulated sugar,
1½ cups of glucose (pure corn syrup),
2 cups of cream,
1 cup of butter,

3 or 4 squares of Baker's Premium
   No. 1 Chocolate,
1½ cups of English walnut meats,
2 teaspoonfuls of vanilla extract.

Put the sugar, glucose, *one* cup of the cream, and the butter over the fire; stir and cook until the mixture boils vigorously, then gradually add the other cup of cream. Do not allow the mixture to stop boiling while the cream is being added. Cook until the thermometer registers 250° F., stirring gently—move the thermometer, to stir beneath it—every four or five minutes. Without a thermometer boil until—when tested by dropping a little in cold water—a hard ball may be formed in the water. Remove from the fire, add the chocolate and nuts and beat until the chocolate is melted; beat in the vanilla and turn into a biscuit pan, nicely oiled or buttered, to make a sheet three-fourths an inch thick. When nearly cold turn from the pan and cut into cubes.

RIBBON CARAMELS

CHOCOLATE LAYERS

1¼ cups of granulated sugar,
½ a cup of glucose (pure corn syrup),
   scant measure,
¼ a cup of butter,
1-16 a teaspoonful of cream of tartar,
1¼ cups of rich milk,
1¼ squares of Baker's Premium
   No. 1 Chocolate,

1 teaspoonful of vanilla extract.

WHITE LAYER

⅔ a cup of granulated sugar,
¼ (scant) a cup of water,
1 cup, less one tablespoonful, of glucose (pure corn syrup),
½ a pound of dessicated cocoanut.

Put the sugar, glucose, butter, cream of tartar and the fourth a cup of milk over the fire, stir until the mixture boils, then very gradually stir in the rest of the milk. Let cook, stirring occasionally, to 248° F., or until, when tested in water or on a cold marble, a pretty firm ball may be formed. Add the chocolate and vanilla, mix thoroughly, and turn into two well-

47

buttered shallow pans. For the white layer, put the sugar, water and glucose over the fire, stir until boiling, then add the cocoanut and stir occasionally until a soft ball may be formed when a little of the mixture is dropped upon a cold marble. Put this mixture over the fire, to dissolve the sugar, but do not let it begin to boil until the chocolate layers are turned into the pans. When the white mixture is ready, turn enough of it onto one of the chocolate layers to make a layer about one-third an inch thick. Have the other chocolate layer cooled, by standing in cold water; remove it from the pan and dispose above the cocoanut layer. Let stand until cold and firm, then cut in cubes; wrap each cube in waxed paper.

FONDANT

4 cups of granulated sugar,	¼ a teaspoonful of cream of tartar,
1½ cups of cold water,	or 3 drops of acetic acid.

Stir the sugar and water in a saucepan, set on the back part of the range, until the sugar is melted, then draw the saucepan to a hotter part of the range, and stir until the boiling point is reached; add the cream of tartar or acid and, with the hand or a cloth wet repeatedly in cold water, wash down the sides of the saucepan, to remove any grains of sugar that have been thrown there. Cover the saucepan and let boil rapidly three or four minutes. Remove the cover, set in the thermometer— if one is to be used—and let cook very rapidly to 240° F., or the soft ball degree. Wet the hand in cold water and with it dampen a marble slab or a large platter, then without jarring the syrup turn it onto the marble or platter. Do not scrape out the saucepan or allow the last of the syrup to drip from it, as sugary portions will spoil the fondant by making it grainy. When the syrup is cold, with a metal scraper or a wooden spatula, turn the edges of the mass towards the center, and continue turning the edges in until the mass begins to thicken and grow white, then work it up into a ball, scraping all the sugar from the marble onto the mass; knead slightly, then cover closely with a heavy piece of cotton cloth wrung out of cold water. Let the sugar stand for an hour or longer to ripen, then remove the damp cloth and cut the mass into pieces; press these closely into a kitchen bowl, cover with a cloth wrung out of water (this cloth must not touch the fondant) and then with heavy paper. The fondant may be used the next day, but is in better condition after several days, and may be kept almost indefinitely, if the cloth covering it be wrung out of cold water and replaced once in five or six days. Fondant may be used, white or delicately colored with vege-

48

RIBBON CARAMELS.
(See Page 47.)

ALMOND FONDANT BALLS.
(See Page 52.)

DOUBLE FUDGE.
(See Page 43.)

ROSE AND PISTACHIO
CHOCOLATE CREAMS.
(See Page 53.)

WALNUT CREAM CHOCOLATES.
(See Page 52.)

ALMOND FONDANT STICKS.
(See Page 51.)

SMITH COLLEGE FUDGE.
(See Page 43.)

CHOCOLATE BUTTER CREAMS.
(See Page 53.)

TURKISH PASTE
WITH FRENCH FRUIT.
(See Page 42.)

MARBLED FUDGE.
(See Page 44.)

FIG AND NUT CHOCOLATES.
(See Page 50.)

CHOCOLATE ALMOND BARS.
(See Page 51.)

CHOCOLATE PECAN PRALINES.
(See Page 42.)

CHOCOLATE POP CORN BALLS.
(See Page 55.)

table color-pastes or with chocolate, as frosting for small cakes, or éclairs or for making candy "centers," to be coated with chocolate or with some of the same fondant tinted and flavored appropriately.

ALMOND CHOCOLATE CREAMS

CENTERS	CHOCOLATE COATING
¼ a cup of blanched almonds, chopped fine,	About 1 cup of fondant,
½ a cup of fondant,	2 squares Baker's Premium No. 1 Chocolate,
¼ a teaspoonful of vanilla,	1 teaspoonful of vanilla extract,
Confectioner's sugar for kneading and shaping,	Few drops of water, as needed, Halves of blanched almonds.

Mix the chopped almonds with the fondant and vanilla; add confectioner's sugar, a little at a time, and knead the mass thoroughly, on a marble or large platter; shape into a long roll, then cut into small pieces of the same size. Shape these into balls a generous half inch in diameter and leave them about an hour to harden on the outside. Put the fondant for the coating and the chocolate (shaved or broken in pieces) in a double boiler (with hot water in the lower receptacle); add the vanilla and the water and beat until melted; take out the spoon and put in a dipping fork (a wire fork costing about ten cents), beat the fondant, to keep it from crusting and drop in a "center;" with the fork cover it with fondant; put the fork under it and lift it out, scrape the fork lightly on the edge of the dish, to remove superfluous candy, turn the fork over and drop the bonbon onto waxed paper. Make a design with the fork in taking it from the candy. At once press half of a blanched almond on the top of the candy, or the design made with the fork will suffice. If at any time the coating be too thick, add a few drops of water. If any be left over, use it to coat whole nuts or cherries.

CHERRY CHOCOLATE CREAMS

CENTERS	CHOCOLATE COATING
¼ a cup of candied cherries, chopped fine,	About one cup of fondant,
½ a cup of fondant.	2 squares of Baker's Premium No. 1 Chocolate.
	1 teaspoonful of vanilla extract,
	Bits of cherry.

Prepare the centers and coat in the same manner as the almond creams.

CHOCOLATE PEPPERMINTS

Melt a little fondant and flavor it to taste with essence of peppermint; leave the mixture white or tint very delicately with green or pink color-paste. With a teaspoon drop the mixture onto waxed paper to make rounds of the same size—about one inch and a quarter in diameter—let these stand in a cool place about one hour. Put about a cup of fondant in a double boiler, add two ounces of chocolate and a teaspoonful of boiling water, then stir (over hot water) until the fondant and chocolate are melted and evenly mixed together; then drop the peppermints, one by one, into the chocolate mixture, and remove them with the fork to a piece of oil cloth; let stand until the chocolate is set, when they are ready to use.

FIG-AND-NUT CHOCOLATES

5 figs,	Powdered sugar,
3 or 4 tablespoonfuls of water or	Fondant,
sherry wine,	3 or 4 ounces of Baker's Premium
½ a cup of English walnut meats,	No. 1 Chocolate,
	1 teaspoonful of vanilla.

Remove the stem and hard place around the blossom end of the figs, and let steam, with the water or wine, in a double boiler until softened, then add the nuts and chop very fine. Add powdered sugar as is needed to shape the mixture into balls. Melt the chocolate, using enough to secure the shade of brown desired in the coating and add to the fondant with the vanilla. Coat the fig-and-nut balls and drop them with the fork onto a piece of oil cloth or waxed paper in the same manner as the cherry bonbons. These may be dipped in "Dot" Chocolate instead of fondant.

CHOCOLATE MARSHMALLOWS

Cut the marshmallows in halves, and put them, one by one, cut side down, in chocolate fondant (as prepared for almond and cherry chocolate creams), melted over hot water and flavored to taste with vanilla. Beat the chocolate with the fork that it may not crust over, lift out the marshmallow, turn it and, in removing the fork, leave its imprint in the chocolate; sprinkle at once with a little fine-chopped pistachio nut meat. To prepare the nuts, set them over the fire in tepid water to cover, heat to the boiling point, drain, cover with cold water, then take them up, one by one, and with the thumb and finger push the meat from the skin.

MAPLE FONDANT ACORNS

2 cups of maple syrup,	2 or more squares of Baker's Premium
1¾ cups of granulated sugar,	No. 1 Chocolate,
¾ a cup of cold water,	1 teaspoonful of vanilla,
Confectioner's sugar,	About ¼ a cup of fine-chopped almonds, browned in the oven.

Make fondant of the syrup, granulated sugar and cold water, following the directions given for fondant made of granulated sugar (cream of tartar or other acid is not required in maple fondant). Work some of the fondant, adding confectioner's sugar as needed, into cone shapes; let these stand an hour or longer to harden upon the outside. Put a little of the fondant in a dish over hot water; add Baker's Chocolate and vanilla as desired and beat till the chocolate is evenly mixed through the fondant, then dip the cones in the chocolate and set them on a piece of oil cloth or waxed paper. When all are dipped, lift the first one dipped from the paper and dip the base again in the chocolate, and then in the chopped-and-browned almonds. Continue until all have been dipped.

CHOCOLATE ALMOND BARS

½ a cup of sugar,
¾ a cup of glucose,
½ a cup of water,
(¼ an ounce of paraffine at discretion),

½ a cup of blanched almonds, chopped fine,
⅓ the recipe for fondant,
3 or 4 ounces of Baker's Premium No. 1 Chocolate,
1 teaspoonful of vanilla.

Melt the sugar in the water and glucose and let boil to about 252° F., or between a soft and a hard ball. Without the paraffine cook a little higher than with it. Add the almonds and the vanilla, mix thoroughly and turn onto a marble or platter over which powdered sugar has been sifted. Turn out the candy in such a way that it will take a rectangular shape on the marble. When cool enough score it in strips about an inch and a quarter wide, and, as it grows cooler, lift the strips, one by one, to a board and cut them in pieces half or three-quarters of an inch wide. When cold, drop them, sugar side down, in chocolate fondant prepared for "dipping." With the fork push them below the fondant, lift out, drain as much as possible, and set onto oil cloth. These improve upon keeping.

ALMOND FONDANT STICKS

2½ cups of coffee A or granulated sugar,
¼ a cup of glucose,
½ a cup of water,
¼ a pound of almond paste,

¼ a pound of Baker's Premium No. 1 Chocolate,
1 teaspoonful vanilla extract,
½ a pound of Baker's "Dot" Chocolate.

Put the sugar, glucose and water over the fire. Stir until the sugar is dissolved. Wash down the sides of the kettle as in making fondant. Let boil to the soft ball degree, or to 238° F. Add the almond paste, cut into small, thin pieces, let boil up vigorously, then turn onto a damp marble. When nearly cold turn to a cream with wooden spatula. It will take considerable time to turn this mixture to fondant. Cover and let stand half an hour. Add the Baker's Premium No. 1 Chocolate, melted over hot water, and knead it in thoroughly. Add at the same time the vanilla. The chocolate must be added warm. At once cut off a portion of the fondant and knead it into a round ball; then roll it lightly under the fingers into a long strip the shape and size of a lead pencil; form

51

as many of these strips as desired; cut the strips into two-inch lengths and let stand to become firm. Have ready the "Dot" Chocolate melted over hot water and in this coat the prepared sticks, leaving the surface a little rough.

ALMOND FONDANT BALLS

Roll part of the almond fondant into small balls. Some of the "Dot" Chocolate will be left after dipping the almond chocolate sticks. Remelt this over hot water, and in it coat the balls lightly. As each ball is coated with the chocolate drop it onto a plate of chopped pistachio nut meats or of chopped cocoanut (fresh or dessicated). With a spoon sprinkle the chopped material over the balls.

WALNUT CREAM-CHOCOLATES

2½ cups of granulated sugar,
¼ a cup of condensed milk,
½ a cup of water,
3 or 4 tablespoonfuls of thick cara-
    mel syrup,

A little water,
1 teaspoonful of vanilla,
¼ a pound of Baker's "Dot" Choco-
    late.

Put the sugar, condensed milk and water over the fire to boil, stir gently but often, and let cook to the soft ball stage, or to 238° F. Pour on a damp marble and let stand undisturbed until cold; turn to a cream, then gather into a compact mass; cover with a bowl and let stand for thirty minutes; then knead the cream; put it into a double boiler; add the caramel syrup and the vanilla; stir constantly while the mixture becomes warm and thin; add a tablespoonful or two of water, if necessary, and drop the cream mixture into impressions made in cornstarch. Use two teaspoons to drop the cream. When the candy is cold, pick it from the starch. With a small brush remove the starch that sticks to the candy shapes. Coat each piece with "Dot" Chocolate. As each piece is coated and dropped onto the oil cloth, set half an English walnut meat upon the top.

TO MOULD CANDY IN STARCH IMPRESSIONS

Many candies, especially such as are of some variety of fondant, are thin when warm and solidify on the outside when cold, so that they may be "dipped" or coated with chocolate. To shape candy of this sort, fill a low pan with cornstarch, making it smooth upon the top. Have ready moulds made of plaster paris, glued to a thin strip of wood, press these into the cornstarch; lift from the starch and repeat the impressions as many times as the space allows. If moulds are not available a thimble, round piece of wood, or the stopper of an oil or vinegar cruet will answer the purpose, though the impressions must be made one at a time.

CHOCOLATE BUTTER CREAMS

2½ cups of sugar,	2½ ounces of Baker's Premium
½ a cup of water,	No. 1 Chocolate,
¼ a cup of glucose,	2 teaspoonfuls of vanilla,
¼ a cup of butter,	½ a pound of Baker's "Dot" Choco-
	late.

Put the sugar, water, glucose and butter over the fire; stir until the sugar is melted, then cook to the soft ball degree, or 236° F.; pour on a damp marble and leave until cold; then pour on the Premium Chocolate, melted over hot water, and with a spatula turn to a cream. This process is longer than with the ordinary fondant. Cover the chocolate fondant with a bowl and let stand for thirty minutes; knead well and set over the fire in a double boiler; add the vanilla and stir until melted. The mixture is now ready to be dropped into small impressions in starch; when cold and brushed free of starch dip in "Dot" Chocolate. When dropping the chocolate mixture into the starch it should be just soft enough to run level on the top. If too soft it will not hold its shape in coating.

FONDANT FOR SOFT CHOCOLATE CREAMS

2¼ cups of sugar,	1 cup of water.
⅓ a cup of glucose (pure corn syrup),	

Put the sugar, glucose and water over the fire and stir until boiling, then wash down the sides of the saucepan, cover and finish cooking as in making ordinary fondant. Let cook to 238° F. Turn the syrup onto a damp marble or platter and *before it becomes cold* turn to a cream with a wooden spatula. When the fondant begins to stiffen, scrape at once into a bowl and cover with a damp cloth, but do not let the cloth touch the fondant. Use this fondant in the following recipes.

ROSE CHOCOLATE CREAMS

Fondant,	½ to 1 whole teaspoonful of rose extract,
Damask rose color-paste,	½ a pound of Baker's "Dot" Chocolate.

Put a part or the whole of the fondant into a double boiler over boiling water. With the point of a toothpick take up a little of the color-paste and add to the fondant; add the extract and stir until the mixture is hot, thin and evenly tinted. With two teaspoons drop the mixture into impressions made in starch; it should be hot and thin enough to run level on top. When the shapes are cold, remove from the starch, brush carefully and coat with "Dot" Chocolate.

PISTACHIO CHOCOLATE CREAMS

Fondant.	⅓ a teaspoonful of almond extract,
Green color-paste,	Pistachio nuts in slices and halves,
1 teaspoonful of vanilla extract,	½ a pound of Baker's "Dot" Chocolate.

Using green color-paste, vanilla and almond extract, mould the fondant in long shapes. Put a bit of nut in each impression, before filling it with fondant. When firm coat with "Dot" Chocolate and set half a pistachio nut on top.

SURPRISE CHOCOLATE CREAMS

Fondant,
Candied or maraschino cherries,
Flavoring of almond or vanilla,

Chopped peanuts,
½ a pound of Baker's "Dot" Chocolate.

Melt the fondant over hot water and add the flavoring. Put a bit of cherry in the bottom of each starch impression, then turn in the melted fondant, to fill the impressions and have them level on the top. Let the chocolate, broken in bits, be melted over warm water, then add as many chopped peanuts as can be well stirred into it; let cool to about 80° F. and in it drop the creams, one at a time; as coated dispose them on table oil cloth or waxed paper

CHOCOLATE PEANUT BRITTLE

1½ cups of sugar,
⅔ a cup of water,
½ a cup of glucose (pure corn syrup),
2 level tablespoonfuls of butter,
½ a pound of *raw* shelled peanuts,

1 teaspoonful of vanilla extract,
1 level teaspoonful of soda,
1 tablespoonful of cold water,
½ a pound or more of Baker's "Dot" Chocolate.

Put the sugar, water and glucose over the fire; stir till the sugar is dissolved; wash down the sides of the saucepan with a cloth or the fingers dipped in cold water, cover and let boil three or four minutes, then uncover and let cook to 275° F. (when a little is cooled and chewed it clings but does not stick to the teeth) add the butter and peanuts and *stir constantly* until the peanuts are nicely browned (or are of the color of well roasted peanuts). Dissolve the soda in the cold water, add the vanilla and the soda and stir vigorously. When the candy is through foaming, turn it onto a warm and well-oiled marble or platter. As soon as it has cooled a little on the edges, take hold of it at the edge and pull out as thin as possible. Loosen it from the receptacle at the center by running a spatula under it, then turn the whole sheet upside down, and again pull as thin as possible. Break into small pieces and when cold coat with "Dot" Chocolate prepared as in previous recipes. Half of a roasted peanut may be set upon each piece as coated. Note that the peanuts used in the brittle are raw. The small Spanish peanuts are the best for this purpose. After the peanuts are shelled, cover them with boiling water, let boil up once, then skim out and push off the skin, when they are ready to use.

CHOCOLATE POP CORN BALLS

1½ cups of sugar,
⅓ a cup of glucose,
⅔ a cup of water,
⅓ a cup of molasses,
3 tablespoonfuls of butter,

3 squares of Baker's Premium No. 1 Chocolate,
1 teaspoonful of vanilla extract,
About 4 quarts of popped corn, well salted.

Set the sugar, glucose and water over the fire, stir until the sugar is melted, then wash down the sides of the saucepan, cover and let boil three or four minutes, then remove the cover and let cook without stirring to the hard ball degree; add the molasses and butter and stir constantly until brittle in cold water; remove from the fire and, as soon as the bubbling ceases, add the chocolate, melted over hot water, and the vanilla; stir, to mix the chocolate evenly through the candy, then pour onto the popped corn, mixing the two together meanwhile. With buttered hands lightly roll the mixture into small balls. Press the mixture together only just enough to hold it in shape. Discard all the hard kernels in the corn. Have the corn warm and in a warm bowl.

CHOCOLATE MOLASSES KISSES

2 cups of coffee A sugar,
⅓ a cup of glucose (pure corn syrup),
⅔ a cup of water,
1 cup of molasses,
2 tablespoonfuls of butter,

¼ a teaspoonful of salt,
4 ounces of Baker's Premium No. 1 Chocolate,
1 tablespoonful of vanilla extract, or
1 teaspoonful of essence of peppermint.

Put all the ingredients, save the salt, chocolate and flavoring, over the fire; let boil rapidly to 260° F., or until brittle when tested in cold water. During the last of the cooking the candy must be stirred constantly. Pour onto an oiled platter or marble; pour the chocolate, melted over hot water, above the candy; as the candy cools on the edges, with a spatula or the fingers, turn the edges towards the center; continue this until the candy is cold enough to pull; pull over a hook until cold; add the flavoring, a little at a time, during the pulling; cut in short lengths and wrap in waxed paper.

WALTER BAKER & CO., Ltd.

ESTABLISHED 1780

THIS House has grown to be the largest of its kind in the world and it has achieved that result by always maintaining the highest standard in the quality of its cocoa and chocolate preparations and selling them at the lowest price for which unadulterated articles of high grade can be put upon the market. Under cover of a similarity in name, trade-mark, label or wrapper, a number of unscrupulous concerns have, within recent years, made attempts to get possession of the great market won by this House, by trading on its good name — selling to unsuspecting consumers goods of distinctly inferior quality by representing them to be the products of the genuine "Baker's." The quantity of goods sold in this way is not so much of an injury to us as the discredit cast upon our manufactures by leading some consumers to believe that these fraudulent articles are of our manufacture and that we have lowered the high standard maintained for so many years. It is difficult to bring the fraud home to all consumers, as those who are making use of it seek out-of-the-way places where deception will the more easily pass.

We have letters from housekeepers who have used the genuine Baker goods for years, expressing their indignation at the attempts of unscrupulous dealers to foist upon them inferior articles by fraudulently representing them to be of our manufacture.

It is a comparatively easy matter to cheapen the cost and give a fictitious appearance of richness and strength to cocoa and chocolate preparations by adding foreign substances and employing artificial coloring matter. The detection of these adulterations, while easy for the expert, is difficult for the cook or housewife.

The safest course for consumers, therefore, is to buy goods bearing the name and trade-mark of a well-known and reputable manufacturer, and to make sure by a careful examination that they are getting what they order.

Our Chocolate and Cocoa Preparations are ABSO-LUTELY PURE—free from coloring matter, chemical solvents, or adulterants of any kind, and are therefore in full conformity to the requirements of all National and State Pure Food Laws.

We have behind us one hundred and thirty-four years of successful manufacture, and fifty-three highest awards from the great industrial exhibitions in Europe and America.

We ask the coöperation of all consumers who want to get what they order and what they pay for to help us — as much in their own interest as ours — in checking these frauds.

WALTER BAKER & CO., Ltd.

WALTER BAKER & CO.'S
Cocoa and Chocolate Preparations

BAKER'S BREAKFAST COCOA
In 1-5 lb., 1-4 lb., 1-2 lb., 1 lb. and 5 lb. tins

is absolutely pure, and no chemicals are used in its preparation. It is of greater strength than cocoa mixed with starch, arrowroot or sugar, and it is therefore more economical.

It is delicious and strengthening.

As a portion of the oil in the cocoa bean has been removed, it is easily digested and admirably adapted for invalids as well as persons in health.

BAKER'S PREMIUM NO. 1 CHOCOLATE
In 1-4 and 1-2 lb. cakes, 1 lb. packages, blue
carton, yellow label

It is the pure product of carefully selected cocoa beans, to which nothing has been added and from which nothing has been taken away. Unequalled for smoothness, delicacy and natural flavor. Celebrated for more than a century as a nutritious, delicious and flesh-forming beverage. The high reputation and constantly increasing sales of this article have led to imitations on a very extensive scale. To distinguish their product from these imitations Walter Baker & Co., Ltd., have enclosed their cakes and pound packages in a new envelope or case of stiff paper, different from any other package. The color of the case is the same shade of deep blue heretofore used on the Baker packages, and no change has been made in the color (yellow) and design of the label. On the outside of the case, the name of the manufacturer is prominently printed in white letters. On the back of every package a colored lithograph of the trade-mark, "La Belle Chocolatière," sometimes called the Chocolate Girl, is printed. Vigorous proceedings will be taken against anyone imitating the package.

Trade-mark on every package

BAKER'S VANILLA CHOCOLATE
In 1-2 lb. and 1-6 lb. cakes and 5c and 10c packages,

is guaranteed to consist solely of choice cocoa and sugar, flavored with pure vanilla beans. Particular care is taken in its preparation, and a trial will convince one that it is really a delicious article for eating or drinking. It is the best sweet chocolate in the market. Used at receptions and evening parties in place of tea or coffee. The small cakes form the most convenient, palatable and healthful article of food that can be carried by bicyclists, tourists and students.

Trade-mark on every package

CARACAS CHOCOLATE
In 1-8 and 1-4 lb. packages

A delicious article. Good to eat and good to drink. It is one of the finest and most popular sweet chocolates on the market, and has a constantly increasing sale in all parts of the country.

Trade-mark on every package

CENTURY CHOCOLATE
In 1-4 lb. packages

A fine vanilla chocolate for eating or drinking. Put up in very artistic wrappers.

Trade-mark on every package

AUTO-SWEET CHOCOLATE
In 1-6 lb. packages

A fine eating chocolate, enclosed in an attractive wrapper with an embossed representation of an automobile in colors.

Trade-mark on every package

GERMAN'S SWEET CHOCOLATE
In 1-4 lb. and 1-8 lb. packages

is one of the most popular sweet chocolates sold anywhere. It is palatable, nutritious and healthful, and is a great favorite with children.

59

DOT CHOCOLATE
In 1-6 lb. and 1-2 lb. cakes; 12 lb. boxes

A high grade chocolate specially prepared for home-made candies, and for sportsmen's use. If you do not find it at your grocer's write to us and we will put you in the way of getting it.

In "The Way of the Woods — A Manual for Sportsmen" Edward Breck, the author, says:

"Chocolate is now regarded as a very high-class food on account of its nutritive qualities. * * * * * A half cake will keep a man's strength up for a day without any other food. I never strike off from camp by myself without a piece of chocolate in my pocket. Do not, however, have anything to do with the mawkishly sweet chocolates of the candy shops or the imported milk chocolate, which are not suited for the purpose. We have something better here in America in Walter Baker & Co.'s "Dot" brand, which is slightly sweetened."

CRACKED COCOA OR COCOA NIBS
In 1-2 lb. and 1 lb. packages, and in 6 lb. and 10 lb. bags

This is the freshly roasted bean cracked into small pieces. It contains no admixture, and presents the full flavor of the cocoa-bean in all its natural fragrance and purity. When properly prepared, it is one of the most economical drinks. Dr. Lankester says cocoa contains as much flesh-forming matter as beef.

Trade-mark on every package

FALCON COCOA

This is a preparation for the special use of druggists and others in making hot or cold soda. It forms the basis for a delicious, refreshing, nourishing and strengthening drink.

It is absolutely pure. It is easily made. It possesses the full strength and natural flavor of the cocoa-bean. No chemicals are used in its preparation.

The directions for making one gallon of syrup are as follows :

8 ounces of Falcon Cocoa,
8½ pounds of white sugar,
2½ quarts of water.

60

Thoroughly dissolve the cocoa in hot water, then add the sugar and heat until the mixture boils. Strain while hot. After it has become cool, vanilla may be added if desired.

The Trade is supplied with 1, 4 or 10 lb.
decorated canisters and 25 lb. drums.
Trade-mark on every package

CHOCOLATE FOR CONFECTIONER'S USE

Liquor Chocolates—plain, sweet, light, medium and dark.
Falcon Cocoa—for hot or cold soda.

Absolutely Pure — free from coloring matter, chemical solvents, or adulterants of any kind, and therefore in full conformity to the requirements of all National and State Pure Food Laws.

VANILLA TABLETS

These are small pieces of chocolate, made from the finest beans, and done up in fancy foil. The packages are tied with colored ribbons, and are very attractive in form and delicious in substance. They are much used for desserts and collations, and at picnics and entertainments for young people. They are strongly recommended by physicians as a healthful and nutritious confection for children.
Trade-mark on every package

COCOA-BUTTER
In 1-2 lb. and 1-5 lb. cakes, and in metal boxes for toilet uses

One-half the weight of the cocoa-bean consists of a fat called "cocoa-butter," from its resemblance to ordinary butter. It is considered of great value as a nutritious, strengthening tonic, being preferred to cod-liver oil and other nauseous fats so often used in pulmonary complaints. As a soothing application to chapped hands and lips, and all irritated surfaces, cocoa-butter has no equal, making the skin remarkably soft and smooth. Many who have used it say they would not for any consideration be without it. It is almost a necessary article for every household.
Trade-mark on every package

COCOA-SHELLS
In 1 lb. and 1-2 lb. packages

Cocoa-shells are the thin outer covering of the beans. They have a flavor similar to, but milder than, cocoa. Their very low price places them within the reach of all, and they furnish a pleasant and healthful drink.

Packed *only* in 1 lb. and ½ lb. papers, with our label and name on them.
Trade-mark on every package

INDEX TO RECIPES

www.ingramcontent.com/pod-product-compliance
Lightning Source LLC
Chambersburg PA
CBHW030112070426
42448CB00036B/760